HOW TO FIND
HEALTH THROUGH PRAYER

◇◇◇

Glenn Clark has for many years been professor of English at Macalester College at St. Paul, Minnesota. Now retired, he edits a quarterly, *Clear Horizons*, and conducts a number of spiritual retreats, "The Camps Farthest Out," over the country. Among his books are: *I Will Lift Up Mine Eyes*, *How to Find Health Through Prayer*, and *Two or Three Gathered Together*.

HOW TO
FIND HEALTH
THROUGH PRAYER

GLENN CLARK

Author of *I Will Lift Up Mine Eyes*
and *The Soul's Sincere Desire*

HARPER & BROTHERS PUBLISHERS

New York   London

CONTENTS

I. BATHING IN THE JORDAN

<><><><><><><><><><><><><><><><><><><><><><><><><><><><><><><><><><>

Parable of the Rotten Apple
in the Sound Barrel

I used to wonder why a rotten apple placed in a barrel of sound apples would make the sound apples rotten, while a sound apple placed in a barrel of rotten apples would not make all the rotten apples sound. I also wondered why a man infected with smallpox when turned loose in a gathering of sound people, would—by his mere presence—make many of the sound people sick, while a sound man walking through a hospital of sick people would not—by his mere presence— make the sick people well.

In other words, I wondered why God, if He were a good God, had made a universe in which soundness and health seemed futile, and rottenness and sickness seemed contagious.

But one day I stopped wondering and examined the so-called sound apple, and I found it was not sound. It was lacerated, torn, wounded to the death. Oh, I know the grocer would contradict me, he would see no defect. He might even sue me for slander if I persisted in spreading the report that he was selling apples that were not perfect. But if he pressed me for proof, I could prove it. I would ask him to look beyond the apple to the stem. There, in the most vital, the most crucial spot of all, he would find the mortal wound that I refer to. He would find that the apple had been torn away from its parent vine, it had been hopelessly separated from its source of life.

When I discovered this, I learned one of the truest facts of life: that nothing, whether it be fruit or vegetable or man, when separated from its source of life is sound!

WHEN NAAMAN WAS COMMANDED TO BATHE
seven times in the Jordan he might well have asked why a
prophet should assume that he had seven layers of dirt and
grime that demanded such thorough ablution as this. Even
the proverbial small boy can usually get down to himself
after three or four scrubbings. Why seven?

It has been my blessed experience in the past few years
to discover how wonderful the fifth, sixth and seventh
bathings can be in the eradication of disease of every kind.
And it is to present the results of my discoveries regarding
these last three inner washings that I am writing now.

The human body is made up of a wonderful series of
layers of flesh and muscle and bone. Sheath is laid upon
sheath with the most cunning workmanship. And the science
of medicine has been moving every century, and recently
we may say, every decade, toward the center of that mystery of what it is that keeps man well. Today we are on
the very brink of discovering the secret of that Elixir of
Life that Ponce de Leon and all those earlier seekers who
limited their searchings to the outer sheaths, failed so
miserably to discover. Medical science, as it gets out its
microscopes and sun rays, is today filled with an optimism
and expectancy that once was possessed only by the ex-
plorers of old. The president of the British Medical Society
said a few years ago, "The conquest of disease is travelling
so rapidly that in fifty years little children will be saying
to their grandpa, 'Grandpa, tell of the time when people
used to get sick.'"

But this enthusiasm, this expectancy, this optimism, can

3

only be brought into fulfillment if we go back to the prophet's injunction and obey it meticulously and understandingly, "Bathe seven times in the river Jordan!"

Since the beginning of time man has been waging a war on disease. All the knowledge, all the understanding, all the science that the world possessed he has brought to bear upon it. Great as has been our success in fighting back disease, why has the success been no greater? Can it be that our arch enemy has employed a strategy which we have not yet learned to meet? Let us bring to bear upon this question our most careful and penetrating thought.

Is it not true that as fast as General Disease—if I may personify him in this way—has been driven out of one line of fortifications he has fallen back upon another and has fought still more bitterly in the second line of defense than in the first? Dislodged from this he has fallen back upon a third, and then the fourth and then the fifth. And in each line he puts up a mightier and deadlier defense than he unleashed in the last. Today he is driven back to the fifth and sixth and seventh lines of battle and never was he fighting with more skill and with more cunning, with more stubbornness and relentlessness than he is fighting today. How are we *finally* and *completely* going to dislodge him? That is the question.

Let me summarize the story of man's battle against disease. In ancient times, and even now in primitive countries, there was much blindness caused by the neglect of washing the babies' eyes upon birth. There were vast numbers of skin diseases caused by lack of washing the skin. Gradually the common science, perhaps we should say the common sense of that day prevailed, and one by one, many if not most, of the simple diseases were washed away. After discovering the value of the outer washing, man soon discovered the value of the inner washing also.

Gradually conditions improved until finally there came the eventful day when Pasteur discovered the great inner trench where General Disease was making his most powerful stand of all, the trench of bacterial diseases.

Through vaccination, inoculation, and antitoxin, modern medical science has made such advances against the enemy on this sector that at times we feel like exclaiming that the battle is won. But, unfortunately, as the enemy withdraws from the trench where bacterial diseases hold sway, he is opening a fusillade of arterial and cardiac diseases, and laying down a barrage of nervous and mental disorders until it seems at times that we are no nearer winning the victory than we were in the Middle Ages. Indeed when we see the insane asylums all over the country, filled to the last room, we sometimes wonder if anything as bad as this ever existed in the Dark Ages. And so we conclude that every advance we have made seems to have been largely nullified by the impenetrable defense in these still deeper inner trenches of the enemy.

If as rapidly as we cure a case of smallpox, a case of cancer breaks out; if as fast as we wipe out yellow fever from the race, nervous disorders sweep over the nation; and if for every case of diphtheria prevented, we find a new case of heart trouble or hardening of the arteries, what good has been accomplished? Have we not been sweeping dust under the rug in one end of the room only to find it blown out into the other end?

Why not sweep out all the dust in the room at once? Why not scrub deep and cleanse all seven layers of ourselves, our hearts and minds and souls as well as our bodies? In other words, why not obey the prophet's injunction and bathe *seven times* in the Jordan?

In the Great War we found that a wonderful transformation had come in the art of attack and defense. Those generals who clung to the old method of open field warfare had to be set aside for the new generals who knew how to use planes and tanks and "pillboxes." Our old methods of attack on the first-line trenches—the shallow temporary fortifications against illness—will not avail against the deeper trenches of the cunning enemy. We must resort to deeper tactics. We must *burrow under* and *rise above*—we must turn to another dimension than the little two-dimensional world in which we have organized our thinking and acting in the past ages.

And what is that other dimension?

To me that other dimension is the spirit. To me, the fifth, sixth and seventh lines of defense are the mind, the heart and the soul.

Let us make an examination of a man as he actually is—the sort of human being that you and I are. First, we find a man with a skin; beneath the skin there are muscles; beneath the muscles there are blood vessels; beneath the blood vessels are organs that create the blood and send it coursing through the body—organs that create and manufacture life-giving elements out of air and food and water. Controlling and correlating those organs are nerves; behind the nerves, a mind; and beyond the mind a great subconscious mind; and behind the subconscious mind a super-mind that controls the Universe.

Let us try to go deeper than the skin and muscles when we want to overcome cancer and mental troubles. Let us go deeper than the organs and blood vessels. Let us go clear through to the thoughts and emotions, the angers and the fears, and let us patiently observe these operating in the subconscious areas of our being. Finally, let us penetrate if we can, to the very citadel of the Holy of Holies—the very Soul of God, Himself, from whence all life comes.

II. THE SEVEN BATHS

◇◇◇◇◇◇◇◇◇◇◇◇◇◇◇◇◇◇◇◇◇◇◇◇◇◇◇◇◇◇◇◇◇◇◇◇◇◇◇

The Parable of the Rivers of Damascus
and the Waters of Israel

*"And Elisha sent a messenger unto him, saying,
Go and wash in the Jordan seven times . . . and
thou shalt be clean. But Naaman was wroth, and
went away, and said, Behold, I thought, He will
surely come out to me, and stand, and call upon the
name of the Lord his God, and strike his hand over
the place, and recover the leper. Are not Abana
and Phärpär, rivers of Damascus, better than all the
waters of Israel? May I not wash in them and be
clean?"*

*Damascus means earthly power at its greatest—the power
that is engendered by the hot, red flames of burning fire,
and by the powerful flow of rich, red blood. "Damascus
steel" symbolizes the finest earth-made weapon known to
man. Saul of Tarsus on the road to Damascus symbolizes
the soul absorbed in material things. Saul's "turning about"
or conversion was the revelation to him that there was a
power from heaven greater than this power which he was
seeking on earth.*

Abana and Phärpär, together, represent the highest mani-

festation of this human power that comes out of the unaided efforts of man. Abana means human stability, or knowledge, at its greatest; Phärpär represents human agility, or skill, at its finest. Together they represent the highest efficiency known to man. What more can one ask than strength combined with agility, science with art, knowledge with skill? If Naaman lived today he would probably reply to a modern Elisha, "Why bother to pray when we have at our service marvelously efficient surgeons and hospital staffs, combining all the sound, substantial scientific knowledge of all ages with the most perfect skills that the human hand is capable of?"

Israel, in direct contrast with Damascus, means "prevailing with the help of the Lord." The Jordan means an "eternal rhythm or constant pounding," and to bathe in the river Jordan flowing through the land of Israel is to submit oneself to the eternal rhythms of the power that is continually flowing out from the heart of God.

Now, taking all of these hidden implications, "to bathe seven times in the river Jordan" means simply to immerse ourselves in the cleansing, healing power of God's love and to put ourselves completely in tune with the rhythms of its flow.

AND NOW WE ARE READY FOR THESE SEVEN immersions in Jordan.

FIRST IMMERSION: WASHING THE OUTER SKIN. Nine tenths of us do not bathe as often as we should. Ninety-nine out of every hundred of us do not brush our teeth as long nor as thoroughly as we should. We do not wash our hands thoroughly enough before eating.

A few years ago the doctors did not wash their hands before operating. Now it has become a rite. Watch a doctor over the basin before he goes into the operating room. He rolls back his sleeves and washes far up on his wrists and arms, much farther than he ever would need to do as far as contact with the patient is concerned. After he finishes washing his hands thoroughly in soap and water he washes them again in some disinfectant. After all these seven scrubbings and immersings he usually puts on rubber gloves besides! Cleanliness is as much the mark of a good surgeon as godliness is the mark of a good clergyman. To that fact, almost more than to the surgeon's skill with scalpel and knife, we owe most of the marvels wrought by modern surgery.

SECOND IMMERSION: WASHING THE INNER SKIN. Washing the kidneys and digestive tract with plenty of pure water is one of the best ways to keep well, and one of the quickest ways to recover health when sick. A sensible internal bathing system recommended to me by a physician years ago is as follows: Drink two glasses of water upon rising, at least an hour before breakfast if possible; again at ten in the morning; and again at two and again at five in the afternoon.

THIRD IMMERSION: CLEANSING THE BLOOD VESSELS. A cleansing of the blood vessels under the skin must be done by washing them, not with water, not with soap, but with blood. Exercise, especially stretching, rhythmical exercise that relaxes every muscle of the body is particularly valuable here. From five to fifteen minutes of stretching and rhythmical calisthenics every day, or better still, twice a day when rising and retiring, and two miles of fresh air "on the hoof" will send the blood on its joyous mission to give this necessary cleansing of the muscles.

To begin the day with ten minutes of calisthenics and end the day with a game of golf or tennis or a two-mile walk in the open air would complete the necessary requirements for proper washing of the blood.

FOURTH IMMERSION: CLEANSING THE LUNGS. An hour of fresh air every day is of infinite value in the cleansing process. The two miles "on the hoof" is partly for the blood stream coursing through the muscles, but primarily for the air stream coursing through the lungs. If housewives, shut up indoors all day, should make it a religious rite not to let one day go by, not even the coldest day in winter, without going outdoors long enough for a good lung cleansing, if merely by a walk around the block, they would make much better wives and mothers. Business men who step from their front yards into waiting cars, then from the cars into office entrances; and who, when work is over, reverse the process, are building foundations for hardening arteries and weakened hearts. Let them leave their cars at home for their wives to use, and walk the five blocks to the streetcar, and if the car is late, walk five blocks more until it overtakes them. Then let them read a book on the way down town that will cleanse their souls.

A business executive found himself a complete physical

and nervous wreck at the comparatively young age of forty-nine. After the clinics had done all they could do for him with medicine and other treatments, he finally went to a physical culturist who specialized in building up broken men. First of all, the physical culturist demanded that he come faithfully to his office three times a week for one month. The next requirement was that he pay him fifty dollars *in advance* for these twelve treatments. The treatments consisted of lying supine on the table, taking a deep breath and holding it in the lower part of the lungs while counting four, then with quick motion lift it to the upper lungs while counting four, then again to the lower for the same length of time, then expelling it and leaving it expelled for the same interval of time. This he repeated over and over again for fifteen minutes. After three days of this the man asked the physical culturist why he couldn't do it at home just as well and not bother to come down to the office.

"Not on your life," exclaimed the other. "You paid me in advance and you have to do it right under my eye. I have found that nine out of ten people are so lazy or careless that they would neglect this unless I supervised them." This lesson was so hammered into him by these twelve "treatments" and by the high price he paid for them, that he formed the habit of going through these exercises every day for the rest of his life. At sixty-nine he was stronger than he was at forty-nine.

FIFTH IMMERSION: WASHING THE EMOTIONS. I have been informed that Freud was once pestered with a persistent, loquacious woman with an incurable disease. She insisted on coming to him at regular intervals to tell all her troubles, and relate all her emotional upheavals to him. He told her frankly that her disease was incurable, and that further consultation would be a waste of time for him and waste of money for her. She said that it was worth what it cost if only to have the chance to talk out what was "on her chest." So on a strictly professional basis he allowed her to talk to him at so much an hour. After a few months he was astounded to discover that she was getting well. Thus it was that the medical profession stumbled upon a method of healing that has revolutionized both psychology and medicine. To drain out the poison from the emotions, it was discovered, is just as important, if not more important, as to drain out the poison from the body. Indeed, is not infection in the soul much more dangerous than infection in the body?

The important thing seems to be to give expression to these infected centers. A man who swears like a trooper when he is crossed will keep in better health than the polite gentleman who pockets his wrath and smiles outwardly. Safest of all, however, is the man who loves instead of hates, and therefore has no wrath to pocket.

In other words the most fortunate is he who has no wrong emotions; next most fortunate from the point of view of health, is he who gives vocal expression to his emotions whenever they come to him. Whether this expression be in the form of quiet, controlled confession to some spiritual counselor or be in the form of violent, uncontrolled expression to the person who caused the emotional upheaval, it does not matter so far as health is concerned.

It is just as bad to lose your temper with yourself and to think mean things of yourself, as to think mean things of others. Indeed, remorse and inferiority complexes are twin causes of many ills. Jesus knew this when He said to the man who was crippled through remorse, "Thy sins are forgiven thee, take up thy bed and walk."

In other words, when one has "dirty" emotions it is better to give them a good scrubbing in the presence of some faithful friend rather than to hide them and hold them in. Only after one has washed his emotions clean can he pray for himself or be prayed for with power.

Take acquisitiveness. When this very valuable trait of human nature gets dusty it becomes covetousness, when muddy it becomes greed, when rusty it becomes miserliness. Cleanse this emotion without destroying it and it becomes a combination of foresight, thrift, and charity—a wonderful trio of virtues.

"Dirty" courage is the gambling poison that has swept many persons into nervous tensions and mental conflicts before their time. "Courage gone to seed" we might well call it. One of the most contagious diseases of our generation today, it is robbing youth and middle age and filling the coffers of gambling barons. Talk of measles and chicken-pox! They don't compare with it, either in destruction of morals and morale, or in destruction of life through break-downs and violent deaths.

Another emotion that requires cleansing in many people is the desire for inspiration, the craving to "step outside one-self," to lose oneself in a power greater than oneself. When properly cleansed, it is the stuff that saints and prophets are made of. When soiled and dragged in the mud, it be-comes slavery to dope and intoxicating liquors. Wash away the deadly craving for fermented *spirits* with the craving for the Holy *Spirit* and we change a common drunkard into a prophet and a seer. Jeremiah called himself a drunkard for God. The one hundred and twenty saints at Pentecost talked with such inspired tongues that those who didn't understand them said, "They are drunk with new wine!"

One emotion that is difficult to keep clean and sweet is the affection for the opposite sex. Wash the selfishness out of "dirty" affections, and lust becomes transmitted into holy love.

Just as blood when washed and cleansed with the life-giving element of water and sunlight brings health to every part of the body, and when sluggish and infected, brings disease, so the emotions when cleansed and in proper circulation, bring health to the body, and when infected and sluggish manifest in illnesses of various kinds.

We should learn in our schools how to scrub our emotions. It is wrong to say that young people have inferiority complexes, or complexes of any kind. No young person has a complex. He may have inferiority *feelings*, but these feelings are not "hardened" into complexes until people become older and get set in their ways. When our feelings gather dirt and become tarnished they become complexes. When we are young a good scrubbing of the emotions fixes us up in a jiffy, but when we grow older these scrubbings may have to be more severe. When one becomes a very old and hardened sinner, a spiritual surgical operation may be required.

SIXTH IMMERSION: WASHING THE MIND. An active, balanced and disciplined mind is one of the greatest sources of health a person can have. Persons of low mentality but of giant physique do not live as long nor keep as well as men of frailer build, who have well-cultivated minds. President Charles Eliot of Harvard was a "blue baby" but he lived into his nineties, chiefly because he had a well-balanced, contentedly occupied mind. Men of wide interests and absorbing application, like Benjamin Franklin and Thomas A. Edison outlive men of narrower interests. This is true also of Charles A. Dana, Immanuel Kant and others, who outlived great athletes like Frank Gotch and Walter Eckersall who had amazed the world by the strength and endurance of their bodies.

People who do not have enough ideas get sick, people who have too many ideas get sick, but people who have the *wrong* ideas get sickest of all. Indeed no man ever said a truer thing than the old philosopher who wrote the proverb: "As a man thinketh in his heart, so is he."

The sickest people of all are the very rich people who do not have enough to occupy their minds. A great nerve specialist told me that the most unhappy people in the world were the unmarried women of very wealthy families who had nothing to do. Another group that needs protection are the people who are out of jobs and need them. Men who retire and have no hobbies to occupy them are a pitiful lot. Another unhappy group includes the people who have jobs but who hate the work they are in, seeing in it nothing but deadening drudgery.

We can approach this subject best by considering first, how our minds can be occupied with our work, then with our play and then with our hobbies.

If a person has no work to engage his mind he should get busy at once to remedy the defect, either by getting a job, or by filling his time in creative, health-producing ways. A person who has work that he hates should either change his field at the earliest possible moment, even accepting work at a lower salary, or, if he cannot change his work, he should change his attitude toward it, seeing all the good in his job which he had overlooked before. The value of a vacation is that it separates a man from his job long enough for him to see it in perspective, and when he returns he often finds in it more sources of happiness and more ways of bringing happiness to others, than he had ever dreamed was possible before.

A good, wholesome *hobby* is one of the best safeguards against illness any man could have. A hobby can often do what one's regular work fails to do—enable him to keep happy in spite of the fact that his work may be filled with drudgery and boredom. Gardening, carpentering, painting, sculpturing, writing, are all wonderful sources of health because they give the mind natural, wholesome outlet, drawing off the old pockets of poison, enabling one to return to his work with a washed and sun-kissed mind.

Next to hobbies come *sports* as a mind cleanser.

The games of life are all health-giving: golf, tennis, bowling, even checkers and chess and bridge. Strange to say there is more danger in sport, like bridge or chess or even golf, becoming too engrossing, than there is that our hobbies shall become our obsession. One never grows morbid over hobbies, unless it might be over some crazy incongruity like a search for perpetual motion, but it is quite possible to get morbid over one's sports. A dowager who plays bridge as though it were a matter of life and death and who criticizes every false move her partner makes, will soon be on the road to the state hospital—or her partner will be. A golfer who makes the air blue with his misuse of the English language every time he dubs a stroke had better take up gardening for his stomach's sake.

Blessed is the man who loves his work, and who also has a hobby, and who also enjoys a good game, and who, above all, has opportunity and time to indulge in all three.

One other way to crowd out wrongs and morbid thoughts is to pack one's mind with good books and reading matter. Keep up on current events with a good newspaper and a good weekly news magazine. Keep in touch with the eternal things of life through good books and masterpieces both new and old.

SEVENTH IMMERSION: WASHING THE SOUL. The soul is a very inclusive term. It incorporates the mind and heart and the entire being, but in a very peculiar and particular way, for the soul is the point at which one's entire being contacts the Infinite. Your infinite self in relation to which your little three-dimensional, conscious Self is but the outer, visible expression, is always well, always sound, always perfect. The trouble is that you do not "live there" enough. "Tell me where you live and I will tell you what you are," someone has said. If you dwell all day long in a countinghouse counting up your greedy gains, or, if you live in a "nagging house," where you have a constant sense of irritation and antagonism with all those about you, or if you live in a "lonely house" where you think of yourself as separate from everyone else in the world, or, worst of all, if you live in a "hating house" where it is "each man for himself and the devil take the hindmost," then you are exposed to all the poisons, all the infections, all the epidemics that flesh is heir to. If you live in high and exalted contact with the Creator, if you are aware of your sonship to the great Father, and if you have a sense of your corporate relationship to your brothers, then you are giving wholesome circulation to the finest part of your being, and the blood, nerves, and organs of your body will manifest the wholeness and harmony experienced in your soul.

To achieve the cleansed soul is to achieve perfection. To achieve this perfection, yes, to come anywhere near it is not to be hoped for in a day, a week, or even a year. To attain it is well worthy of a lifetime of effort.

Health is an old English way of spelling wholeness. And wholeness is merely a modern, scientific way of spelling holiness. To give oneself wholly to God and to practice continually the presence of God is the only sure short cut I know of to achieve holiness—which in turn is the only short cut I know of to achieve permanent, undeviating health. To attain completely this perfection of the cleansed soul is too large an order for this book to attempt. I would refer you to my books *I Will Lift Up Mine Eyes* and *The Soul's Sincere Desire* which were written with just that end in mind. The actual application of this inner holiness of the Soul to the act of healing the outer body, however, is the central theme of the chapters which follow.

III. I GO FORTH ADVENTURING

◇◇◇

The Parable of the Lightning
That Struck from Below

Once upon a time a man thought he would protect his house from the lightning in the skies by attaching a lightning rod to the chimney on his house. But to his amazement his dwelling was the first one in the city to be struck. After he had rebuilt his house, a stranger came and sojourned with him one night and, learning of his previous misfortune, counseled him thus:

"Do you not know that lightning is not confined to the skies alone? It abides everywhere. It is in the ground under your feet as well as in the clouds over your head. The next time you raise a lightning rod to the skies, also sink another lightning rod into the earth."

This the man did, and ever after his home was protected.

Many years later the man fell ill of a disease that his physician said no human remedy could cure. But because the physician was a man of faith he said, "The only thing that can help you now is Divine aid." But because the man had no faith in anything outside of this world he at first refused to act upon this advice. Weeks went by and his health continued to grow worse. Finally he could not leave his bed and so one day he wrote to a man of prayer and begged him to do what he could to help him.

The man came and sat by his bedside, took his hand and said, "God is not limited to my prayers nor to my presence, nor to any one church, nor to any one creed. God is everywhere. He abides in you as well as He abides in me. You have been reaching up to others for help; now sink your shafts of faith down into yourself. Establish ground wires to the Eternal Source of Life that is within you knowing that It is ever present, ever powerful, and immediately available whenever a real need calls with a faith that is sincere."

Then the man remembered another time when a stranger had said to him, "Do you not know that lightning is not confined to the skies alone? It abides everywhere. It is in the ground under your feet as well as in the clouds over your head."

So he obeyed the words of the man of prayer and soon found a reservoir of power that he had never dreamed existed before, and in time became sound and well. Then one day he opened a book that had long remained closed upon his desk, and in it he read, "Thy faith hath made thee whole."

WHEN MY EARLY DISCOVERIES IN PRAYER FIRST came out in book form in *The Soul's Sincere Desire*, I was besieged by requests from all over the country for prayers for healing of the sick. At first I shrank from asking God to harness his giant Niagara of the Spirit to their little mill wheels of the body. But one day after spending hours over the New Testament it dawned upon me that two thirds of Jesus' reported acts were acts of healing, and from that time forward I consented to pray for the body as well as for the soul. But I did lay down one condition—that discipline of the mind and heart and soul should always precede the prayer for the body. For I agree completely with Dr. Loren T. Swaim of Boston who wrote me, "I think there are too many miracles demanded without any real disciplined living or real hard work behind them. When Jesus found the real faith plus the disciplined living and a responsible person, He could cure at once. I think sometimes we have to be prepared to be cured, so that it is really worth while doing it." Having made this discovery and having laid down this condition I at once decided that before I started disciplining others I had better start disciplining myself. This chapter, therefore, shall be the story of how I disciplined myself.

I found the first bath—cleansing the outside of the body —and the second—cleansing the inside of the body—were pretty well taken care of in my general routine. The third bath—exercise to cleanse the blood stream—would have been rather sadly neglected had I not had the foresight to build my home a half-mile from the college where I teach. My schedule required that I cover the distance four times a day, fall, winter and spring. By adding a few calisthenics to my daily routine this requirement was pretty well taken care of. As I advance in years I have become a great believer in the rhythmical, stretching type of exercises which I prefer to the more vigorous forms of calisthenics.

In experimenting with the fourth—washing of the lungs— I made an interesting discovery. When very tired I discovered that deep breathing, especially in the open air, was very refreshing but did not completely relieve me of my fatigue. The most complete rest, next to sleep itself, could be mine if, after I had *exercised* my lungs awhile I *rested* them. This rest process consisted of relaxing the body completely and then *exhaling* and not inhaling again as long as I could refrain in comfort. If I came very fatigued to a speaking engagement I found that even while sitting on the platform before hundreds of people that I could rest my heart and lungs by lengthening the periods before each inhalation. In the five or ten minutes before the time for me to speak I could be entirely refreshed.

But when I came to the fifth, sixth and seventh baths I began to get into trouble. My *pièce de résistance* was my mind. Ordinary wash cloth and ivory soap wouldn't work here. I had to resort to the stiffest kind of bristled brushes and the strongest kind of tar soap. I am naturally a doubting Thomas. I cannot act on a thing unless it meets the tests of common sense and sound reasoning. If you wish to witness some of the scrubbing I gave here it is:

I found it hard to make my mind believe that actual, concrete, definite body conditions could be changed by such an intangible, ephemeral thing as prayer. It was hard for me to make my mind believe that anything besides physical means could remove physical obstructions. If a person is really and truly sick there can be no make-believe about it.

How can one who is in his right senses and not a complete idiot assert, there is no sickness, all is health? If a person has cancer, he has cancer, and there are no two ways about it.

Indeed, even today, my mind is still insisting just as it did before on a rational explanation for everything just as far as that explanation can be forthcoming. But, thanks to a mighty good scrubbing my mind now accepts the sweet reasonableness of the power of prayer to bring health to a suffering body. And this scrubbing of the mind occurred not before some mystic or occult shrine, but right in the working laboratories of Western science.

In the physics and chemistry laboratories we find that the body is not a solid thing, it is fluid; it is not permanent, it is changing every hour, every minute, every second. Moreover, the physicists tell us, that even the little solidity which we *think* the body possesses is illusion. We all know that the body is three-fourths fluid, but the scientists go even farther than that. They tell us that all solid body structures are made up of molecules, which in turn are made up of atoms, which again are made up of electrons, and these electrons are themselves nothing but opposing points of force. Professor Sir William Crooks, one of the greatest living chemists said before the Authors' Club of England on December 5th, 1910:

If we had just established the idea of the fixity of the old-fashioned elements, we would say we still had matter to fall back upon. But philosophers have not respected even the sacredness of matter itself. Physicists are now beginning to say that in all probability there is no such thing as matter; that when we have caught and tamed the elusive atom and split it into 700 little bits, these residual particles may turn out to be nothing more than superimposed layers of positive and negative electricity. I refrain from speculating as to what would happen to us if some clever researcher of the future discovered a method of making the alternate layers of plus and minus cancel each other out!

In the light of that statement, perhaps Jesus, Elijah, and the nine others who are recorded in history and legend to have ascended into heaven without dying, knew the secret. If a man could gain such control over his body that even the atoms would respond to his slightest wish, all he would need to do would be to command the negative and positive layers of electricity in each atom to come together in such delicate juxtapositions that they would cancel each other out, and his body would "dematerialize" instantly from the sight of man. It sounds absurd, but almost as unbelievable things have happened in our own time—such as voices carrying a thousand miles through the ether—and we accept them as daily facts. However, while we cannot go so far as to conceive of a body becoming invisible (except through an X-ray) we can accept the fact that the body is not a solid thing, but a point of energy revolving about a cohesive idea —of *you* or of *me*—held together in perfectly adjusted and harmonious relationship through the co-ordinating power of our inner individual soul.

Thus, by a good scrubbing in the actual laboratories of physicists and chemists, I began at last to see my body as a fluid, flowing, aerial thing, changing every hour, every minute, yes, every second, according to my least mood, my lightest idea, my most superficial thought. Into this fluid, flowing thing every idea that I ever thought—after I was through with it—and every emotion—even before I had recognized it and even after I had forgotten it—was dropped. If not given complete expression and cast aside, these emotions and thoughts lay there as seeds bringing forth fruit after their kind.

But while the mind bath was the hard one for me, I found that nine times out of ten the emotion bath was the hardest for most of the people that came to me for help.

In my own particular case I simplified this bath by reducing my emotions to two fundamental ones and concentrating on them: anger and fear. I found that Dr. Horace Fletcher was right when he said some years ago that these two emotions are the parents of all the vices. Anger is the parent of all the masculine vices; fear is the parent of all the feminine vices. As it is discouraging to attempt to rid a house of flies when there are ten thousand of them, but easy where there are only two, so I plucked up courage, picked up my swatter and got to work on the two flies that had been messing up my life. The way I overcame anger and its little offsprings of jealousies, grudges, bitterness, and unforgivenesses, was to make a practice of seeing every human being as a perfect being in a perfect world governed by a perfect God. The first chapter of Genesis says that man is made after the image and likeness of God. I soon found it entirely possible and very reasonable to look at *God's* handiwork, man, with the same respect with which I looked at *man's* handiwork in a radio factory. When my radio poured forth terrible music I didn't destroy the radio, I just tuned in to another station. When my child had tantrums, I didn't strike him, I simply tuned in his radio to another station.

Because I always held this view of man as a perfect image of God, naturally innocent, sweet and pure, I never suffered the pangs of hate, and by the use of this "leverage" I was enabled to free hundreds of bitter souls from the poison that was blasting their lives.

I was not so fortunate, however, when it came to fear.

I was a very imaginative child, and had the misfortune of being entrusted to the care of nursemaids who used terror as a means for securing obedience. Bad boys who wouldn't obey their elders might find strange creatures unexpectedly coming out of cellar closets or making nocturnal visits to those who hadn't said their prayers. Some aunts whose chief recreation was recounting their husbands' last illnesses visited us often. One old wives' tale that impressed itself upon me more than any other was that of a man who awakened one bright morning to find he had gone blind. As a child, I found myself waking in pitch darkness and stumbling to the window to find whether I could see the stars.

I was in my early thirties when a strange palpitation of the heart came upon me night after night converting my periods of rest into periods of torture. Each night I went through the whole gamut of dying. No matter what remedy was used the condition persisted. If I worked hard in the daytime to drive away the dread of night, hoping to induce sound sleep through great fatigue, it was all to no avail. To work under such tension made it worse. To loaf and save myself was equally useless. As the years went on and the condition continued to baffle the doctors, I decided I must use the Baths of Jordan.

All emotion of fear must be *completely* washed away. Perhaps some forgotten childhood fear induced by some old wives' tale had left a seed, which, if found and removed, would effect a complete and an immediate cure. And there I learned an important lesson—that it is often very difficult to find the initial, subconscious cause of a present problem. Failing in that, I took another course. I went back to the root of all fear, yes, of all anger, of all vices that flesh is heir to—to the root cause of all—to *self*.

The application of this to my own state required that I

be perfectly willing to let God take me into death if he wished, without any concern whatever as to what He did with this little, insignificant body of mine. So night after night when the palpitation began, instead of feeling my pulse, fighting for breath, and wondering how long my heart could stand the pounding, I tried to discipline myself to saying, "Smash up if you want, old heart, I can stand it as long as you can."

I thought I noticed a little improvement, but it was very slow. Then a call came to me to speak for a week to the Rocky Mountain College Y. M. and Y. W. C. A. Conference at Estes Park, Colorado, 8,000 feet above sea level. Another call came for me to attend a three-day conference of the American College Quill Club at Laramie, Wyoming, 7,000 feet above sea level. Heretofore I had carefully declined any calls to high altitudes. I spent three days in Denver once and my heart had palpitated night and day without letup. In high altitudes it seemed as though the old ticker raced with the speed of an engine with its governor belt off. Because I knew that my family needed me and because there surely must be important work for me to do in the world, I felt that I had no right to risk my life. So the invitation was declined. I went to the Midwest College Y.M.C.A. Conference at Lake Geneva, Wisconsin, however, and led a group of college boys for ten days. When the camp was over "Dad" Elliot said to me, "I don't see how you have a moral right to decline any sincere, earnest call to speak at camps like this when God has given you such an authentic and special message to speak to your fellow men."

That remark remained with me and would not let me rest. A month went by. Finally I sat down and wrote the Rocky Mountain Conference secretaries that I would come.

I went in the same spirit that a soldier would volunteer

to lead the "forlorn hope" across no man's land to rout out a machine-gun nest in the face of a withering shower of lead. When I said good-by to my wife and children, my eyes lingered long on their faces. I didn't know whether I would ever look upon them again in this world.

I went because God, speaking through the Rocky Mountain secretaries, was asking it. I went because God, speaking through "Dad" Elliot, was commanding it. Whether my family needed me, or whether I had more work to do for the world, that was not for me but for God to decide. If He snatched me away before His work was done, that was not my hard luck, that was God's hard luck. I did not belong to myself, I belonged to God and His kingdom, and if He needed me He was capable of taking care of His own. God was the arbiter of my destiny.

In that spirit I went. In that spirit I led the Prayer Hour before breakfast each morning. As the sun came over the mountain peaks, I threw back my head and looked into the sky, realizing as never before how God speaks to us through His handiwork. Words were not really needed in those hours; they seemed trivial intrusions upon the mighty silences of God.

Every morning was a Mount of Transfiguration. After a while God began to speak through me with almost the same power that He was using to speak through the mountains. It was as though each morning some new revelation was born. People asked me the secret of it. The secret of it was this: those mornings of Transfiguration were but the fruitage of the nights of Gethsemane that preceded them.

The very first night that I reached Estes Park palpitation seized me as usual about two in the morning. I looked about the strange room and then remembered—I was up on a high mountain. The words of my hostess returned to me, "We have given you a room away from the other leaders, so you won't be disturbed." How kind it was of her to place me where I could not even knock on the wall and call a companion to come to my help if I should need help! The Lord certainly had "placed me far out on a limb." To God and God alone I could turn in my hours of need.

I went to the open window. Outside the moon made everything as bright as day. Framed in the window sash was a view of a high mountain, remote, snow-capped and gleaming in the moonlight.

"I will lift up mine eyes unto the hills," I said slowly. "From whence cometh my help? My help cometh from the Lord who made heaven and earth. You made me, Father," I said. "I am more wonderfully made than any mountains. If You want to take me—take me. If You want to preserve me You can easily preserve me. I leave it entirely to You, O Lord. You decide it. I am your man."

Night after night, instead of getting worse, my heart was eased. When I returned from Estes Park the palpitation and even the tendency toward it had gone. I was as one liberated from a sentence of death. And so I found that the way to save one's life is not to run away from death but to face death fearlessly. He that loseth his life shall find it.

This, then, is the great remedy, the quick remedy, the only *sure* remedy that I know of. But it is very hard to teach others how to use it. It is rather extreme treatment I admit for a patient to apply to a toothache or a mild cold, for instance, to be willing to lose his life. It is a cure that cannot be applied at a moment's notice. It comes only after months or even years of spiritual growth and discipline.

Therefore, I found it best in quick situations to wash out the *particular* blockage and *then* pray for healing. But I discovered that even this was often more difficult than we would imagine. To find the roots of wrong thinking behind the particular disease is often the most baffling of all tasks. As in my own case where I found it so hard to find the initial fear that planted my harvest of palpitation, so I often found it still harder to find the initial cause in others.

Is there, really, any connection between our bad thoughts and the bad health of ourselves and of our loved ones?

One day a woman came to me with a confession that started me on a long and interesting quest to answer that question. She was a woman close to eighty, who had lived a full life of rich service ministering to the needs of the poor. "How can you account for the seeming cruelty of God?" she asked. "I married, not for love, but because I desired children. I had three. But one by one as they reached the age of four they all died. How can you account for a Father of Love doing that to me?"

After a pause, she herself furnished the answer. "Did God do this because there is some law that children can only be brought permanently into the world by the price of genuine, sincere love of man and woman?"

Some years later when I was in another city, a woman asked me to pray that she would love her husband more. "You see, for years before I married him I was intensely in love with another man. He married another woman and so I married Percy, but I cannot completely erase the yearning memories of that first love. But Percy also married me on the rebound after the girl he wanted to marry married another man."

"Do you have any children?" I asked.

"Yes, a fine boy and a fine girl. But before they came I lost two babies by miscarriage. Can it be that the secondhand love I was giving my husband, and the secondhand love he was giving me was not strong enough to bring those first children safely into the world?"

One day I saw in the paper an account of two children burned to death by an accident that only could have occurred once in a thousand years. As I read on I found that the parents were divorced and an intense bitterness existed between them. Since then I wondered if children of parents who hate each other to the extent of wishing the other was dead are in danger of unexpected accidents?

My own son, when a small boy, often spent hours on our slippery roof stringing wires for radio aerials. It always made me a little nervous to hear him sliding around on the housetop. My wife said, "Don't let that bother you. I feel sure that if we keep on loving each other with a high, strong love no harm can touch him."

One day she and I were engaged in a rather heated discussion over a subject where we had very different opinions. Upstairs we could hear the attic window open and our son's footsteps pattering out onto the roof. Both of us were startled at the sound.

"Glenn," exclaimed my wife, "ask him to come down till we finish this argument."

I smiled, but because I could see the point, I hurried outdoors, and called to him to come down for a minute.

Then I hurried in and we quickly brought our discussion to a happy ending. As we were finishing, our son appeared on the stairs landing above us, and asked, "What do you want me for, Dad?"

"Nothing now," I said. "Go back to your aerial," and we turned our smiling faces toward him.

"Hey! What's the big idea?" he exclaimed.

That is the question that I am asking my readers. Is this a big idea, or is it foolishness? One thing I can say for it, at any rate, and that is that any family that tries to keep sweet and harmonious and happy within itself will certainly reap many harvests far more worth while than the mere harvest of health.

I advance it merely as a hypothesis and advance it with this qualification:

If it is true that bad thoughts and bad emotions are reflected in bad health, and that hate thoughts become boomerangs upon those we love, then we certainly have the Grace of God to thank for tempering justice with mercy. Most of us would have suffered far worse than we have, had the Lord exacted the full measure of justice.

My final discovery was that people who hate and who fear are essentially selfish people. "The trouble with me," said a woman to a famous psychiatrist, "is that I am very sensitive."

"Yes, I see that you are very selfish," was the reply.

"You didn't hear me right," she corrected, "I said sensitive, not selfish."

The psychiatrist smiled. "Are not selfishness and sensitiveness the same thing?"

When one learns to forget himself he ceases to be afraid. When he learns to forget himself, there is nothing to be angry for. "Have you ever been snubbed?" someone asked Alice Freeman Palmer. "Oh, yes," was the quick reply. "Many times. But it never bothered me because I never was there."

If you are not there you will not get angry; if you are not there you will not get afraid; if you are not there you will not get sick. Let us take the prescription of Emily Dickinson and make it our own:

I'm nobody; who are you?
Are you nobody, too?
Good, then there's a pair of us—don't tell!
They'd banish us, you know.

How dreary to be someone!
How public, like a frog,
To tell your name the live-long day
To an admiring bog.*

* From *The Poems of Emily Dickinson*, edited by Martha Dickinson Bianchi and Alfred Leet Hampson. Reprinted by permission of Little, Brown and Company.

IV. WASHING OUT THE ROOTS

<><><><><><><><><><><><><><><><><><><><><><><><><><><><><><><>

The Parable of Invisible Bacteria, and the Secret Fear

Once upon a time, a man, seeking rest and relaxation from the pressing cares of life, went into a moving-picture house. There he soon became fascinated with the unfolding drama of a little bearded chemist of Paris who startled the doctors of his day with his experiments with bacteria. Finally a famous physician demanded of him, "Do you mean to say that you expect us to believe that something ten thousand times smaller than a flea can kill a man!"

The next day the man could not get this picture out of his mind. He went to a physician of his acquaintance and said to him, "Would it be possible that the discovery of Pasteur was not the end but just the beginning? Is it possible that something ten thousand times smaller even than bacteria might be more potent than bacteria in killing a man?"

The physician smiled. "You think you have made a new discovery but you have not. It is a well-known fact that over half our bed cases in our American hospitals are of mental and nervous origin. We physicians all know that fear, anger, selfishness, greed and jealousy are just as dangerous as Pasteur's disease-causing bacteria."

The man was silent for awhile. Then he said: "But Pasteur went so far as to ascribe different types of bacteria as the cause of different types of diseases. If Pasteur were experimenting in this field today would he not ascribe a different type of mental or emotional maladjustment as the root cause behind every disease?"

The doctor smiled. "That opens a new and interesting field for research. If one entered upon it as Pasteur did with an open mind, offering his facts at first not as facts but merely as hypotheses, there would be nothing to lose and everything to gain in giving this theory a good trial. Its proper application need not require the dismissing of the family physician, nor the taking of untried quack drugs, nor the submitting to experimental operations. It would require only a thorough discipline of the soul. I doubt whether any of my patients would not benefit immensely—physically, mentally and spiritually—from a thorough discipline of the soul."

I SINCERELY BELIEVE THAT WRONG THINKING has much to do with bringing disease upon us. But I do not wish to imply, by any means, that those who are the worst invalids are consequently the worst sinners. Indeed, I believe, that very often just the contrary is true. For I have discovered that it is the most spiritually sensitive, the very highest and finest souls amongst us, who suffer reaction from wrong thinking much more quickly than the thicker-skinned brand of humanity. Therefore, illness is not so much a sign of special shortcoming as it is an indication of definite, spiritual sensitivity. As swine can grub in the mud and eat fermented garbage without immediate attacks of indigestion where a deer would die of such food in a few days, so there are types of mankind, who can wallow in the mire of sin without getting the immediate reaction that more spiritual souls may get from letting a little congestion with self touch the hem of their garment.

With this preliminary statement, which should make clear that no one need feel particularly disgraced if he finds himself coughing before he gets through reading this chapter, let us look below the surface and try to find the roots of the various diseases.

In the last chapter I related my discovery that selfishness or the thought of self was the old, evil grandfather from which all our brood of diseases spring, and that anger and fear were the father and mother. Therefore, if one were to be free from disease all he would need to do would be to rid himself of these three particular vices. But as that is a pretty large order, not something that can be accomplished in a day or a week, I propose that we endeavor to find what form of wrong thinking may be the cause of *each* particular illness so that each patient may concentrate upon removing that one specific cause.

In *I Will Lift Up Mine Eyes* I describe a friend who had great power in healing others through prayer because he insisted upon seeing the bodies of himself and of his friends as expressions of the Spirit of God. To him our personal bodies were only receiving sets for manifesting the perfect love, truth, and joy of God through our channels of consciousness.

If one were sick my friend did not see a sick body, he saw a perfect receiving set catching a message from the great broadcasting station of God, and the moment the message was decoded and obeyed, instantly the sickness would vanish. Is it not true that when you have answered the telephone call, the bell ceases to ring? And is it not just as reasonable to believe that sickness itself is merely a vibration set up in the sensitive responses of our marvelously responsive body, which will cease as soon as we reverently put the receiver to our ear and promise to obey the command that is being sent?

I, personally, know that some of the most effective, direct messages that God has ever sent me, He has sent in the form of temporary illnesses. One message was that I was to take more time to be still with Him. Another time He told me that I must throw out all my worthless baggage of fears. When colds come to my friends I tell them that they are simply personal messages from on High to cease being congested with thoughts of self. Many of our ills might be traced to criticism or cynicism gone to seed—and so on and on. Indeed, I hardly know how I should get along in this world if it were not for the frequent use of this marvelous receiving set, which is called the body and which the Father has provided for keeping me in continual touch with His steering hand in my life.

What is the message that each particular illness may be trying to convey to us? Let us see if we can get still and read the code. For convenience I shall divide all our ailments into groups or families. Let us begin with

I. THE GROWTH FAMILY

A. BENIGN GROWTH

A woman with a goiter and tumor came to me. She was so physically and so nervously run down that her doctors did not consider an operation safe. There seemed no door open but the door of prayer. So I rolled up my sleeves, figuratively speaking, and went to work.

"If you had a Ford car," I said, "and your neighbor had a Cadillac, even though you knew in your heart that you had no need of a larger car, nevertheless, because you were so eager to 'keep up with the Joneses' you kept wishing for a Cadillac, presently you would get a Cadillac. For everything we want hard enough and long enough ultimately comes to us. But when you put your Cadillac in your garage you find your garage is too small, and the car sticks out about two feet. Let us call this 'sticking out' a 'growth.' Now let us see if you can recall anything you ever wanted which was not evidently meant for you in your Divine Plan."

She thought a long while and finally remembered one thing she once desired so greatly that it made her actually sick to find she never could have it.

"But it was so long ago I had forgotten it," she added.

"Well, never mind how long ago it was. Just pick it up, roots and all, and throw it out the window. Then take this little Divine Plan I am handing you and read it every morning for six weeks."

She complied faithfully with my directions and in six weeks she reported. "The doctors said my goiter and tumor, both, are disappearing, and I won't need an operation."

From this and other experiences I am inclined to believe that those afflicted with growths of any kind should pull up their yearnings for unrealizable achievements and give them utterly to God. Contentment in the state where they are is the surest cure they could find. Very often such growths mean nothing more than a highly developed inferiority complex—that morbid habit of seeing what others have achieved with yearning regret over one's own weakness. When I see such sweet and lovable souls suffering from this affliction my whole heart goes out in longing to see them made well.*

B. MALIGNANT GROWTH

A woman came to me from Oklahoma on her way to the Mayo Clinic at Rochester for an operation. She especially wanted my prayers as some of her friends were certain that it was a malignant growth. I asked her if she ever had a bitter thought toward anyone. After a half-hour's conversation I knew that I rarely had met anyone so completely free from resentful thoughts toward others. I asked if anyone had done any injustice to her in the past, which had left some half-forgotten bitterness rankling within. She had, of course, suffered her share of injustices and mistakes in life, but always she had set these aside as a part of the game and held no ill will even for a moment against anyone who had caused them.

* Any one desiring a copy of this Divine Plan may obtain it by sending fifteen cents in stamps to the Macalester Park Publishing Company, St. Paul, Minnesota, for a copy of the booklet *The Lord's Prayer*, in which it is contained.

"Go to Rochester for your operation," I said, "but I can assure you that the surgeons will find nothing but a very mild and innocent growth." A letter a week later confirmed my diagnosis.

As envy is often associated with benign growth, jealousy is often associated with malignant growth, but chiefly when the jealousy is accompanied by injustice that creates resentment.

Let me say that one who suffers cancer is no big sinner; he is far more often the innocent victim of some other sinner, some cruel or unjust employer or unfair and betraying friend.

Cancer victims are nearly always perfect "ladies" and "gentlemen," the kind who, if they have a grudge, are too "ladylike" or "gentlemanly" to give vocal expression to it. With lovely self-control they bury it out of sight, not knowing that, like the fox which the brave Spartan youth concealed beneath his garment, it might eat away their very liver. Swearing men rarely die of cancer. They die of apoplexy instead. The chief sin of the cancer victim is often his *politeness*, which prevents him from confessing his grudge to some father-confessor. If he cannot "*cuss*" and if he cannot *confess* there still remains one avenue open for cure—the best avenue of all: He can *forgive* and *forget* the one who wronged him.

A neighbor of mine had cancer of the throat. Her physicians could do nothing for it. She went to the greatest specialists in the country. They told her there was no hope. She turned to faith healers with still no results. Finally, a friend asked her, "Is there anyone you have a grudge against?" She replied, "There is one person that I hate so hard that it makes me sick all over just to think of her." Then the friend said, "You will have to forgive that person before any prayer can help you." This the woman positively refused to do. When her husband came home that evening she told him what her friend had said, and he, because he loved her very dearly, made her kneel down beside him in their room and kept her kneeling all night, till she finally consented to forgive the one she hated. From that hour she began to recover. Today she is one of the healthiest and happiest women in America.

II. The Rheumatism Family

A. RHEUMATISM

For rheumatism, dig down and see if you can find any trace of cynicism, skepticism or criticism. Rheumatism has an affinity for other "isms," it seems. When you can find the particular "ism" that seems most dominant in you, dig it up and throw it away, and the ministrations of your physician and the prayers of your friends will have amazing healing power. But if you hang onto any of these three little disease germs of the mind, you will find the grip of your illness is very stubborn indeed.

I once was called to Rochester to see a very dear friend who had a peculiar case of rheumatism that required a long period of observation, and which mystified the doctors completely. As I visited with him and recalled what a dear, big-hearted man he was, and what immense trust he had in human nature, I asked him if anything in life had changed that trust. He said, "No," that while he had run up against many things that might have made the ordinary man cynical or critical or skeptical, nothing had ever changed his kindly attitude toward all men. After an hour's casual, friendly conversation with him I was so convinced that he had not a single "root" from which rheumatism could grow that I said flatly, "I can assure you without question or doubt that when the doctors have finished their examination of you they will announce that you haven't rheumatism at all." And sure enough, the doctors soon discovered that they must look for another cause, one which they soon found, something very unique, which, had it not been discovered in time, might have proved fatal.

B. ARTHRITIS

I find that all arthritic invalids are people of extremely strong characters. They are, indeed, usually the salt of the earth. For a long time it was a mystery to me why arthritis attacks the strong, original, pioneering, patriarchal type of folk which the world especially needs as leaders, until I learned one day that their very strength of purpose, their very unswerving conscientiousness, their very rigidity of will were their own undoing.

This rigidity of will becomes destructive when, instead of pressing forward on some creative purpose, it turns aside and forces itself to do something which at heart it does not want to do. Stubborn rebellion might also be a cause. When one refuses to reconcile himself to losing a loved one, or holds back from associating with people by whom he is surrounded, the arthritis condition sometimes manifests itself. One chief cause of arthritis is our attempt to pack too heavy a program into too small a space, or to achieve too definite and perfect results in too short a time. Time and Space are the metaphysical spine and ribs which hold our universe within the bounds of Form, but even they have their limits, and when these limits are exceeded, ankylosis is liable to set in.

The best cure is to forgive all, relinquish all, and surrender all. If one can do the thing he really wants to do, and can drop responsibility into the hands of God, even as the clay rests in the hands of the potter, much can be accomplished by the prayer that follows.

III. The Circulation Family

A. THE HEART

Poets from time immemorial have associated the heart with the capacity to love. Accepting that as our cue, let us look behind all troubles of the heart to see if we can remove any inhibitions of the affections or any limitations in one's capacities to love. Children raised in homes where there is a tendency to criticize others, or even where there is a "choosy" attitude in regard to those who should be loved are apt sometimes to manifest difficulties in the action of the heart. As most homes are more or less that way, it is only by the grace of God that we do not all suffer from heart trouble.

Very few of us can live up to Jesus' standard in the Sermon on the Mount of forgiving our enemies and doing good to those who despitefully use us. Nevertheless, I have seen seemingly serious heart conditions righted in a marvelous way, when the one so afflicted learned how to love everyone without discrimination and without limit.

B. BLOOD VESSELS

As the capacity to love is associated with the heart, joy, flowing through the channels of consciousness, is associated with the blood that flows through the arteries and veins. Nothing quite so much as joy can regulate circulation. The birds are the most joyous of creatures and they have a blood circulation that completes its circuit every two minutes. Joy steps up the chemical activity of the body; its subtle effect upon the iron-bearing foods causes pale red cells to become deep red cells and, therefore, is the best preventive there is against anemia. It is amazing how many illnesses are cured by the simple action of joy.

When young people suffer from anemia it is because they are not having enough fun in life. Even though they may be on the go constantly—to. theaters, movies and dances—and to all appearances are having lots of fun, almost invariably it will be found that the heart is unsatisfied and their ceaseless activities are simply an "escape" to hide their secret hunger for true happiness.

People shouldering great responsibilities in social affairs, entertainments and sports which ordinarily are considered "fun" but for them must be "work," are especially in danger of anemia. Football coaches for whom play is work, college presidents for whom social gatherings are a prelude to soliciting endowments, actors, especially comedians whose job it is to be funny, are particularly inclined to anemia.

But just as anything which converts our relaxations into responsibilities, and our fun into toil, reduces the hemoglobin or iron content of the blood, so, on the other hand, anything which increases our joy of living, especially anything that converts our toil into fun, increases the health-giving hemoglobin immensely.

If anemia tends to manifest where there is a shortage of happiness, high blood pressure is likely to appear where there is an overabundance of that which kills happiness, such as monotony, anger and worry. Nothing is worse for high blood pressure than despair or tantrums of temper. The more one can let God shoulder the heavy responsibilities of life, and the more one can take life sweetly and calmly, the more completely one can check or relieve this ailment which is growing to be one of America's most common plagues.

Man is said to be just as old as his arteries. The chief cause of arteriosclerosis is the living of old thoughts over and over again. The best preventive and cure is the inflow of new thoughts, especially life-bringing thoughts of love and peace and happiness.

IV. THE DIGESTIVE FAMILY

The power to assimilate food easily seems closely related to the power to assimilate ideas.

Great literary movements have often centered and flourished around coffee houses or dining clubs. The literary geniuses of Sam Johnson's day revolved around the coffee taverns of London and the dining room of Mrs. Thrale; of Victor Hugo's day around the dinners of George Sand; of our own New England School of authors around the Parker House Club. Great authors are often great connoisseurs in regard to food.

A person with a good, clear mind usually has a good, clear digestion. But as nothing interferes with straight thinking more than fears and worries, and as nothing interferes with one's capacity to reason soundly and accurately as much as impatience, hot temper and prejudices of all kinds, so fears, worries, angers, and prejudices have a tendency to reflect very quickly in the digestive processes.

A. MINOR DIGESTIVE TROUBLES

Misunderstandings play havoc with one's digestion, especially misunderstandings between people. Impatience, which is merely refusing to take time to think, is bad for the digestion. Temper, which is the outgrowth of impatience, is still worse. Fear can give anyone dyspepsia, particularly fears that are due to misunderstandings or to the inability to see ahead and know how things are going to turn out. Worry, which is synonymous with ignorance and fear of the unknown and lack of trust in God, is probably the most senseless, the most unreasonable thing there ever was. A little sound understanding of what worry is all about and how foolish it is, should do much to wash it away.

Diarrhea and nausea are most likely to occur where there is a sense of disgust and repulsion. The former reflects one's consciousness regarding a past occurrence, and the latter reflects one's reaction to a present or future one. It is actually a cleansing process, and if one finds the definite psychic thing that bothers him and "confesses it out" and achieves a sense of forgiveness regarding it, it is amazing how quickly the trouble can be cured.

Holding back ideas, or failure to express them, due to shyness, diffidence, or undue secretiveness tends to cause constipation. Inhibited persons are usually the worst sufferers. Far better than physic is the removal of shyness and inhibitions to effect a cure. Where one is debating about some difficult decision over a long period of years, actual blockages, serious in nature, are apt to manifest. A young woman I know, who spent five years debating within herself whether she loved a suitor well enough to accept him, was positively plagued by chronic states of blockage in her digestive tract.

B. MAJOR DIGESTIVE TROUBLES

The stomach seems to be related to the *immediate assimilation* of ideas; the liver to the more *permanent organization* of ideas, such as lead to the forming of judgments. Just as the liver of the codfish extracts and stores from sunned foods the ultra-violet rays of the sun so the spiritual counterpart of the liver in the soul of man extracts the deeper and the more subtle and penetrating truths of God. Hence, confusion that leads to harsh, unkind judgements or deep-seated jealousies against people over a long period of time may manifest in trouble in the liver.

Although I knew that stones symbolize money in allegorical literature, nevertheless, I have been surprised to find how often stones in the liver or kidneys have come to those who are puzzled or confused over their ideas of giving, either of money or of themselves. Especially to be guarded against is resentment growing out of the suspicion that others are imposing upon you or trying to exploit you. A state of "chronic unhappiness" or frustration continued over a long period of years, especially when growing out of misunderstandings and wrong judgements sometimes "congeals" into stones in the liver. A different type of frustration manifests in stones in the kidney.

The kidney represents the capacity to purify the ideas and the emotions of life from overthought of the self. The need may be to purify the sex impulse, but far more often to purify the *self* impulse.

The pancreas represents the sense of far-reaching encompassment. A man who has gluttony for food or a great thirst for power or for fame, or even for serving mankind, may find that when these satisfactions are suddenly shut off that diabetes appears. It seems that when the sweetness from the outside world is taken away that the inside world works overtime to provide it. Some of God's greatest souls with the most encompassing influence for good, go through life with this affliction.

Ulcers in the stomach are directly related to the worry that rises from a sense of inadequacy. Hence, it oftens afflicts persons placed in positions of responsibility.

Typhoid fever is related to both the digestive tract and the nervous system. It comes from drinking polluted water when one's physical resistance is low, and, on a psychological plane, it may reflect emotions polluted with fear, jealousy, doubt, and conflict. The skin eruptions and diarrhea that often accompany the disease might be called the desperate effort to free the body from these death-dealing "emotion" germs.

V. THE NERVES AND MENTAL FAMILY

A. NERVOUS TROUBLES

Our nerves are our channels in consciousness, and anything which blocks the smooth, harmonious flow of God's free life through our channels of consciousness tends to disturb the nervous system. Obstructions and frictions tend to produce jars. A girl struggling between two decisions, to marry the man she loves or to stay dutifully by a mother who needs her care, may some day become a nervous wreck. Prolong this strain unduly through the years and she may become a mental case.

There is nothing harder on the nerves than a struggle within oneself over two choices. Such struggles are like the jars that shake down the house. If the struggle continues long enough it divides one's nature into two separate selves. If the struggle between these two opposing natures cannot be reconciled it results in a "split-personality" and the neurosis passes into a psychosis. Physicians, by medicine, rest, diet and proper nursing, attempt to restore balance and harmony to the mental and physical functions.

Strange as it may seem, this is exactly what prayer also achieves on a more ethereal and higher plane. Prayer creates harmony within the soul of man which in turn is conveyed in vital and perfectly normal ways through the entire system. By making oneself wholly surrendered to God, by ending all two-pointed loyalties, half to God and half to this world, one puts oneself in the place where all internal subconscious struggles for supremacy cease, and harmony and balance are restored.

There is nothing so effective for bringing one into balance as an actual application of believing prayer, especially if continued patiently and persistently by a loving and loyal husband or wife or other close relative through the months and the years.

Those who suffer from nervous troubles are usually highly organized, finely textured individuals. Delicately balanced main springs of watches can easily get out of order, but when properly running they are the finest instruments there are. A nervous type of individual can just as easily become the most sensitive and valuable channel through which God may perform His greatest works. If one can accept the hypothesis that nerves and glands are "channels in consciousness," any one who is a "bundle of nerves" might make himself just one big channel of God's consciousness, and find that at the same time he has made himself into a remarkable channel for God to do His work through him.

B. MENTAL TROUBLES

When a neurotic condition becomes psychopathic we speak of it as a mental unbalance rather than a nervous unbalance. A psychopathic person lives in two worlds, partly in this one and partly in an ideal one which he has created. We might simplify it by saying that he is obsessed with a partial view of life, has surrendered his whole being to it. This is what was called in Jesus' day, being possessed by demons.

I have found praying as Jesus must have prayed very effective in cases like this. That is, by determining what the obsession is and personifying it in one's mind, and then commanding it to depart. A partial view or divided view of life is *always* inferior to a whole view, and therefore must of necessity be obedient to it.

VI. Skin and Membrane Irritations

A. SKIN ERUPTIONS

Skin eruptions or irritations of any kind are often outer expressions of inner sensitivity to environment. Whether this is eczema, hay fever, or sinus trouble depends upon the nature of the person affected and upon the nature of the peculiar stimulus that is offensive to him. Physicians already have discovered that those afflicted with these lesions are usually allergic to certain foods, certain types of outer stimuli, such as goldenrod, roses, or ragweed. They may soon discover that persons with the same affliction may be allergic to emotional and mental environments as well. For every flower or weed to which a person's skin is allergic there probably is some type of person (or experience) to whom his soul is allergic.

One person may be irritated by his work, another by the idiosyncrasies of a person who works beside him in the office, another by an unwelcome suitor, another by a nagging mother, another by an irresponsible husband or wife.

Getting at the inner causes should be the first step in attempting to cure such troubles. Merely to move into a new environment, to leave the town where the disagreeable relative lives, sometimes effects a cure. To change one's inner life, however, so that nothing and no one offends any more, is, of course, by far the best.

B. MEMBRANE IRRITATIONS

In some people these irritations manifest in outer eruptions —skin rash, eczema, etc., and in others they manifest inwardly as in hay fever, asthma, etc. I do not know the reason for this differentiation, but I should be very interested to find out from someone who has compared a sufficient number of cases.

Sinus trouble, as well as adenoids and enlarged tonsils, usually afflict people who have a set determination to succeed. Consequently, sinus trouble is most frequently found in leaders or people who like to have their own way or who are older or more set in their ways. Babies often have eczema, but rarely have sinus trouble. Beyond that I do not feel prepared to go. I know that sinus trouble especially affects persons of strongly ambitious and leadership abilities, and asthma afflicts people who are touched with self-pity. Therefore I am inclined to believe that the outer skin irritations are more apt to affect those who tend toward being extraverts and the internal membrane irritations are more apt to afflict those who tend toward being introverts.

VII. The Rhinitis Family

A. THE COMMON COLD

The common cold might well be called an outward manifestation of the common selfishness to which we all are subject. A cold is attended by congestion, and who of us has ever experienced a more virulent congestion than that of "too much self." It is my conviction that the common cold is an expression or outpressing of the commonplace, trite sins of life, such as little irritations, little worries, little fears, little jealousies, little lusts, little conceits, little vanities, which destroy the natural defenses against infection. If anyone wonders at my listing fears and worries among sins, let me remind him again that these are the offspring of the greater sin of *doubting* God. But I find that merely the thought of self, uppermost in most of our minds most of the time, is the chief and central cause. A simple attack of perfectly innocent self-consciousness is enough to give some young, sensitive people a good attack of wheezes.

The best protection against contracting the common cold is to forget oneself as completely as one can, to think lovingly of others, to read good spiritual literature and to surrender oneself as completely as one can to God.

B. THE SERIOUS COLD

When the wrong thinking is intensified by hidden, suppressed fears, or by great overwhelming jealousies or lusts or angers, they become more dangerous. When respiratory infections become very dangerous, as the Spanish influenza did during the World War, which claimed twice as many lives as the battlefield claimed, it is due, I contend, to a great inflooding of wrong thinking and wrong feeling of entire nations. The flood of hate and fear in the last stages of the first World War was like an act of pouring poison into the very air which men breathed. Luther Burbank was right when he said, "The day is coming when people who throw out hate and anger and jealous thoughts into the air will be considered just as dangerous to society as people who throw poison into wells."

In the case of serious pandemics such as influenza at its worst, the best protection is to let go any suppressed fears, to forget and forgive enemies of one's nation, and put oneself completely and trustingly into the hands of God.

Pneumonia is more apt to occur where there is disappointment, discouragement, or a sense of frustration of some kind. When this is so extreme that the subconscious is deeply affected to the point where (without the person himself knowing it, perhaps) he would like to get away from it all, the sickness sometimes takes a fatal turn in spite of all the doctor's care.

Tuberculosis is often manifested where this frustrated yearning, usually a yearning for affection has been experienced for years, so long, indeed, that it may actually have been forgotten by the conscious mind. This forgetting is what often makes it difficult to find immediately the psychic cause.

Tonsillitis and quinsy often represent a lifetime of repressed fears and disappointments which have packed themselves into one's tonsils, which stand as kindly guardians to keep all such discordant things away. They are physical and spiritual filters, to filter out all the inharmonious things, spiritual as well as physical, that threaten to enter into one's being. When these guardians become too packed we have them out, without as much as a kindly "thank you" for all the evil they have saved us from in the past. After one has his tonsils out, he should immediately appoint in their stead, two spiritual guardians to protect him against further attack —the spirit of love, and the spirit of peace—and he will be immune from all of such trouble in the future.

VIII. Children's Illnesses

A. MILDER DISEASES

Children under twenty, strange to say, are affected as to their health far more by their parents' wrong thinking than by their own. Discuss the justice of this all you wish, I simply state it here as a fact. These milder diseases represent the outbreak upon the children of the milder forms of selfishness and wrong thinking of the parents. They usually are called "necessary diseases," but, in my opinion, the reason they are necessary is because few parents are entirely free from the little, minor faults and flaws that flesh is heir to. For instance, chickenpox occurs frequently where there is oversensitivity and petty irritations regarding environment; measles finds a soil in irritations and anger; whooping cough may appear where there is repressed vanity and self-pity; and mumps is possibly associated with over-repression or expression of the sex impulse.

These "necessary diseases" will cease to be necessary, I firmly believe, when we have a more perfect race of men and women. But it will be some time before we can be saints. It is highly important, however, for parents, when faced with the emergency of a sick child, to take counsel together and to highly resolve, at least for the time being, to observe a lenten period against indulging in any of the little, minor sins, especially the sins of quarreling, nagging and general lack of harmony. Such a mutual resolve may do as much to bring immediate healing as all the doctor's remedies in the world. If you do not believe it, the next time your child gets sick, put it to a trial.

B. MORE SERIOUS CHILD AILMENTS

Scarlet fever, diphtheria and smallpox are not called "necessary diseases," and the reason may be that it is not necessary for the parents to experience the more violent expressions of wrong thinking. Scarlet fever is likely to appear where there have been explosions of temper, anger, or deep bitterness against people. Diphtheria is sometimes associated with intense fear and self-pity. Smallpox may be caused by a sense of great fear, great inferiority, or great resentment against society.

Parents are far too little aware of how deeply and how quickly their own mental states react upon their children. I have known of a terrific burst of temper on the part of a parent to be followed the following week by scarlet fever hitting his child. I have known of a strong desire on the part of a man to give his enemy a smash on the nose to be followed by his own child falling and getting a tremendous blow on the nose. Of course, these might be called "coincidences," but a doctor, when confronted with a child who cannot talk at the age of five, will almost invariably tell the parents to over-come any tension that exists between them, before he can attempt to promise any cure for the child.

And yet we must not let this frighten us, or we would none of us have courage to bring children into the world. It is, however, a challenge to us all, and should induce in us a greater appreciation of the values of religion and the prac-tice of holiness than most of us ever suspected.

IX. Accidents*

Is it true that persons are partly responsible for the acci-dents in life that befall them? Is it not true that a man who desires to be sympathized with and babied by a wife he thinks indifferent is more liable to be knocked down by a passing car and brought home in an ambulance than the man who has no such desire? A man who wishes he could "knock his rival's block off" and suspects his rival of conspiring to knock *his* off is far more likely as far as I have observed, to stumble when crossing a street and have the pavement come up and hit him than the man who doesn't have these pugilistic de-sires. As a matter of fact, when I was younger and more pugilistic, the asphalt street and I had several such collisions directly traceable to these causes.

* I had written what follows before Mr. Gray's article in the June, 1939 *Harpers* was published, informing me of Dr. Flanders Dunbar's examination of 1300 cases which seems to verify my hypothesis that accidents are effected by our thinking.

There is one law that I have never known to fail: *Hate boomerangs!* If a woman hates her daughter-in-law and wishes she were dead in order to have her son back again, she may awake some day to find that this hate thought has boomeranged, missing the daughter-in-law, and striking her own son.

I wish to take this opportunity, however, to sweep out any superstition in the power of "black magic" or "malpractice" upon innocent people. No evil thought of another can have any power over you, except the power you give it. Superstitious natives in Africa and in the South Sea Islands give great power to the evil thought of others, hence when a medicine man puts a voodoo spell upon them they are as good as dead. Anyone who understands the law of the subconscious, knows that it is not the medicine man, but their own fear that kills them.

On the other hand, I can say with even greater emphasis that anyone who attempts to practice black magic on another will sooner or later find that the evil thoughts will boomerang back to his own home to destroy him and his house. Our sins, no matter whether in thought or in action, always come home to roost.

X. ADDICTIONS

1. SMOKING

Looking at the smoke addiction first—the little chickenpox among the greater vices—we have the actual statistics of people who have carefully investigated that two thirds of those who smoke suffer from it seriously. Of these two thirds, most at one time or another *try* to break themselves of the habit. One half of these usually accomplish it and quit; the other half go on helplessly crippled by their habit all the rest of their lives.

Smoking comes from the desire for quietness, the desire to get still, to be calm and poised. That is the germ of good underneath the desire. There is, of course, a mixture of many desires such as pride, self-importance, audacity, courage, vanity, desire to be debonaire and dashing that help to sustain it. But underneath is this one good desire—to be poised and still. To overcome this habit, try to develop the capacity to get still with a beautiful book in your hand instead of a cigar, try to sit in silent prayer with a group of friends instead of with a pipe in your mouth, or try to stand in silent meditation with a great work of nature, instead of a cloud of cigarette smoke, filling your eyes.

2. DRINKING

Alcoholic appetite springs from the desire to step outside of self—in other words, to be inspired. The desire to touch Pentecost is hidden in every human soul, an experience which led those who saw the one hundred and twenty to say, "They are drunk with new wine." If one could get opportunities to find inspiration through reading inspiring books, through doing his work by inspiration instead of by routine, he would open legitimate and safe avenues for expressing this craving which would lead to exchanging his dependence upon alcoholic spirits for a reliance upon Almighty Spirit.

I have found that men whose lives are subject to routine and monotony in their business, or routine and monotony in their homes tend to take up this habit, in fact, are driven to drink faster than men in more inspiring environments.

3. SEX

The sexual desire springs from the craving for oneness, the earthly manifestation of the most celestial and purest of all aspirations given to man. But just as the reflection of the highest peak of the highest mountain reaches down to the lowest depths of all reflections in the lake at the mountain's foot, so the highest of all motives of man can find the most degrading manifestation when given wrong expression upon this earth. A real spiritual awakening, a new environment and new association with high and superior souls where love can manifest in highest terms can sometimes convert the lowest of wrecks into the most wonderfully purified of souls.

4. GAMBLING

With the closing of the frontier and the regimentation of so much modern life in formal education and work in factory and shop, the opportunity for adventure approaches the vanishing point in modern living. Gambling has substituted a spurious and morbid doorway for this expression. Not until the church and the school open new doors of adventure in the fields of intellectual and spiritual and social discovery will we find a sure cure for this affliction which today bids fair to be the most flagrant of all the modern sins of men.

5. LYING

Lying comes from the desire for perfection. To create a perfect world, or to create in the eyes of others a perfect self without the labor necessary to deserve that perfection, is the chief cause. It is the perfectionist imagination gone haywire. It often develops into an addiction in a young person who has been long repressed, browbeaten, cowed under a sense of inferiority and guilt, until he is driven to violent extremes to create for himself a better world. It is an escape into a dreamworld for the timid and lazy souls who feel that they have been deprived of the happy world that their hearts desire.

The quickest way out of this habit is to learn the power

and mystery of prayer at its finest and best. In time the one with the lying addiction will find himself living in a real Kingdom of Heaven on earth which so surpasses his spurious make-believe one that no longer will he be tempted to substitute falsehood for the truth. He shall find the truth and the truth shall make him free.

6. STEALING

The thief has a matrix for abundance which, by misuse, has gone to seed. One can raise a squash in a few months; it takes ten years to grow an elm tree. A person who is tempted to steal is rebellious against the slow processes by which God's supply and abundance are coming to him through the humdrum paths of work and industry. He should memorize John Burroughs' poem, "Mine Own Shall Come To Me," put himself under a spiritual advisor or a father-confessor, and report openly any dishonest thing he does, yes, even the dishonest thoughts and temptations that come to him, and ask to have them prayed away. He should learn at once that taking that which is not his own closes the door and keeps from coming to him the much greater riches that *are his own.*

Let me repeat, I have found over and over again that the person who steals has what I call a matrix for drawing money to himself, and if he stops the habit of stealing and learns how to trust God, and lay hold of Him in prayer, he will be surprised and will surprise his friends by the way financial success comes to him. It may sound strange, but if I could get into my employ an army of reformed thieves, truly repentant and really reformed, who have learned how to pray and sincerely look to the Lord for guidance and help, I am sure that any business I undertook would prosper.

Take any vice, cleanse it in the water of penitence and

surrender and purify it with God's sunlight of Love and Joy and you will find one of God's most precious virtues. Jesus took Matthew, the publican, and Peter, the liar, and built a religion that has swept around the globe.

WHY SOME PEOPLE DON'T WANT TO GET WELL

I mentioned that the spiritually minded are the most responsive to the vibration of mind, the ones who are quickest to catch the reaction called illness. There are some grounds to congratulate oneself on one's capacity to become ill. It speaks well for one's spiritual sensitivity. Yes, there is some basis for the old adage that "the good die young." But while the spiritually minded, because they are the most spiritually sensitive, are the quickest to get ill, they also are the easiest to pray for and the quickest to recover from their illness.

Spiritual people are easy to pray for—unless they don't want to get well. But who in thunderation wants to stay sick, I can hear you ask. More people want to be sick than any of us realize. First, there was Paul, the founder and organizer of the Christian Church. He did not want to get over his defective sight, and why? Because wherever he went preaching the gospel of Christ, there were in his audience scores of widows and orphans, whose broken homes were the mute evidence of his own ruthless persecutions of their husbands and fathers in those years preceding his own conversion. Paul did not want to see those faces, he did not in his own mind even want to recall those scenes. He wanted blindness or partial blindness, not only to keep away those scenes, but also to make some small atonement for the evil that he unwittingly had done.

Another who did not want to get well was Edison, who refused to submit to an operation which might have restored his hearing, for fear that the capacity to hear the people who sought his attention might interfere with his work which was so dear to his heart. I know a woman bound to her bed and chair with arthritis, who, previous to her illness, was unpopular in her village, unsought, unappreciated, and who now has found her bed a veritable throne, drawing scores of kindly, solicitous friends who never before were aware of her presence.

Yes indeed, it is positively amazing how many people want to stay sick, and still more amazing how many people actually want to die. Perhaps you have noticed how many people fade away from almost nothing the moment they cease to have something worth while to live for.

A man in the pink of health loses an only son. Shortly afterward he contracts a mild illness, which in spite of all the doctor's care, soon enters into a very difficult stage, and to the surprise of everybody, soon carries him away. A girl is disappointed in love, contracts a strange disease, and in spite of the prayers of all her friends, soon passes away.

I often have startled friends or relatives of a very sick person who persists in growing no better in spite of the best doctors' science, best nurses' care, and the most devout praying, by asking, "Does he really want to get well?" "He says he does," is usually the reply. "But, stop to think of it, I recall now that for the last year whenever he reads of the death of one of his friends, he says, 'Well, there is another lucky one who doesn't have to worry about the stock market.'"

In all cases where a sick person is in a stubborn and continuing illness when there is no special reason for its long continuance or for the dangerous turn it is taking, it is well to find out what the patient holds in his deep subconscious mind, possibly even something he is not consciously aware of, which makes him subconsciously seek a "way out of it all."

V THE WAY JESUS HEALED PEOPLE

◇◇

"Without a Parable Spake He Not unto Them"

"These works—these mighty works, these miracles, if you will—are the direct outcome of Jesus' converting everything that He saw into parables. And a parable, we find, is merely 'an allegorical relation of something real.' Looked at from this angle, the performing of a miracle is not such an impossible task. It consists merely of looking at Reality through the lens of the imagination, and then letting this parable, or imaginative way of looking at Reality, bring to pass that thing which is spoken of as a miracle.

"And what is Reality? Reality, in the eyes of the practical man, is made up of cold, hard facts. And what are the hard, cold facts of life? As we look about us in this world what we see all too frequently are the quarrels, bickerings, unhappiness, unfaithfulness, treachery, covetousness, and materialism everywhere. These are the facts of life. But what are facts? Fact comes from the word factum, *meaning something that we do or make. Are these facts of life identical with the realities of life? Not according to Jesus. To Him Reality does not consist of that which is* made, *but of that which eternally* is. *Love is—quarrels are made; joy is—*

unhappiness is made; truth is—*lies are made;* life is—*sickness is made. So Jesus went through life seeing no quarrels, no unhappiness, no lies, no impurity, no sickness. Where they appeared to be He turned the lens of His divinely inspired imagination upon them; He converted them into parables, and behold, they stood forth revealed as mere shadows or reflections—upside down—of the reality. And every time that Jesus converted a fact into a reality the people exclaimed that a miracle had been wrought.*"—The Soul's Sincere Desire.

YOUNG PLAYWRIGHTS ARE TOLD TO USE Shakespeare as an inspiration but *not* to use him as a model, as his methods so transcend the methods of ordinary writers that it would be folly to attempt to imitate them. In some of his earlier plays, however, where his pen had not yet attained the scintillating magic of later years, one can detect at places the faint outline of his technique showing through; and it is therefore to these earlier plays that the young playwright should go if he wishes to imitate Shakespeare at all.

As Shakespeare is the unmatched genius in the literary world, Jesus is the unmatched genius in the spiritual world. The miracles that Jesus performed were done with such ease and such celerity, that the methods he used defy analysis. Like a great baseball pitcher who throws the ball with such lightning speed that we hardly can see it, or a great football player who breaks through the line in such marvelous ways that we cannot follow the play, Christ furnishes so great an inspiration and an ideal for us, His power is so transcendent and beyond us, that we despair of following in his footsteps.

If we undertook to help a person spiritually we would probably have to hold a long, long conference with him; he would probably analyze his problem to us, then we would quote scripture to him, pray with him, advise him, perhaps lay our hand upon him. Jesus did not even have to take time to pray. He merely said, "Take up thy bed and walk," or, "Thy faith hath made thee whole," or sometimes the sick one had only to touch the hem of His garment as He was going by and she was cured.

We certainly cannot ever expect to be able to attain such spiritual power as that, even though Jesus did say, "Greater works than I have done shall ye do, because I go to the Father."

Where, then, can we go to discover Jesus' method of healing people after a fashion that our slow steps can follow?

Fortunately, Jesus has left for us one example and one example only of what I might call a "slow-motion, close-up" view of His technique of healing people who were sick. At every other point in his active ministry his method was so invisible to our slow eye and dull brain, that it baffles all attempts of the average human being to imitate. Careful study of this incident in all its remarkable details will present a perfect model for us to follow with confidence and assurance that we are following in the right path. In this incident we shall find a perfect restatement in a living, dynamic form of all the philosophy of healing that the preceding chapters have deviously and clumsily attempted to present. I shall invite your careful attention, therefore, to a detailed interpretation of the ninth chapter of the gospel of St. Mark.

"After six days Jesus taketh with him Peter and James and John, and leadeth them up into a high mountain apart by themselves."

"Six days thou shalt labor," says the Scriptures, and ever since that phrase "Six days" has always stood as a symbol of good honest work. The most effective periods of prayer are those that are preceded by periods of work. Whether that work is active service among people, or whether it be intensive, painstaking study into the facts and laws of spiritual life as you are doing right now, it doesn't matter very much. Suffice to say that our high moments of prayer come, not out of loafing and neglecting our duty and daily responsibilities, but they grow out of facing life's hard realities with faithfulness and honest toil. Woe unto us, however, if we become so engrossed in our routine tasks of hand and brain that we forget to take the time to go apart once in a while and pray. As a climax to any serious piece of hard work there should always come a place and time for prayer.

"Jesus leadeth them up into a high mountain."

"Hill" and "mountain" in the Bible always are symbolical of prayer or the uplifted thought. "I will lift up mine eyes unto the hills." That this was a particularly high period of supreme prayer for Jesus is indicated by the use of the word "mountain" instead of "hill," and by the addition of the adjective "high" besides. At no other place in the New Testament is the combination of words, "high mountain" used, as far as I know.

"Jesus taketh . . . Peter and James and John . . . apart by themselves." The highest moments of group prayer come only when we have a carefully selected group who are perfectly in tune with us, and who are willing to "go all the way" with us. These three were the only ones of the twelve that Jesus could count on to ascend to the highest understanding of prayer. It is all very well to enlarge our prayer groups to take in the beginners, the stumbling novices. When we are merely studying *how* to pray we should never deny them the opportunity to learn and share with us the benefits of any spiritual inspiration that we may possess. But in times of extreme need, when we come together to pray with all the power we have for some situation that demands *all* our capacities for prayer of the highest type, then it is our duty to take into the inner closet with us only those who are completely in tune with each other and with us and who possess unquestioned faith in the power of the healing love of God.

But supposing one goes alone into the "secret place of the

Most High," and does not have three spiritual friends available to go with him, how does this chapter help us there? In that case I suggest that we look into the spiritual symbolism that these three disciples represent. In Dante's "Paradiso," Peter represents Faith, James, Hope, and John, Love. When you wish to enter into the holy experience of prayer at its very highest take with you only these highest attributes of your mind and soul: Faith, Hope and Love, and deposit all the ballast of your mind and heart, such as fears, doubts, angers, jealousies, lusts and greeds, down at the mountain foot.

How wonderful our prayer becomes when Sacrificial Love, Unfaltering Faith and Unconquerable Hope combine together to produce it! Such a prayer can fill the Universe and resound to the inner throne of God, Himself.

Now this "Communion with the Father" on the mountaintop does not consist of prayer only, for one would weary and his attention lag if he spent an hour or even fifteen minutes in improvising prayer after prayer. Such communion would defeat itself by becoming mechanical. When you enter into your "Quiet Time," it is well to take a few books along, or at the very least, the Bible, for you will find the need at such a time of two kinds of nourishment. First, a statement of the laws of God's power phrased in ways that will make you realize if possible that God's power is greater than the laws of gravity and the laws of the tides. Second, a collection of poems and prayers or of inspired prophetic discourses that will lift your vision to the very stars. The LAWS will furnish foundation and firmness to your belief; the PROPHETIC literature will furnish inspiration and radiant power to your belief. Thus fortified in the Quiet Hour, you will be ready to emerge into any situation, no matter how difficult, with the light of victory shining in your face.

Jesus entered so completely into this experience of the Law and the Prophets that they ceased to be merely books of wisdom in that hour, and manifested in the living forms of Elijah and Moses, themselves. This indicated more convincingly than a thousand words of proof could do, that the Law and the Prophetic teachings were not dead letters but were living experiences to Jesus. Peter would have rested satisfied in that hour, and with that purpose in mind, exclaimed, "Master, it is good for us to be here: and let us make three tabernacles; one for thee, and one for Moses, and one for Elias." Jesus knew better. Such a transcendent experience was merely preparation for the more humble and loving experience of helping His fellow men.

"And His raiment became shining, exceeding white as snow; so as no fuller on earth can white them."

After one has drawn apart from the world, taking only his highest attributes of the soul with him, and after he has, through meditation upon the Law and Prophets, been lifted into high communion with God, things begin to happen to him. His own body, which is the garment of his soul, grows more light in weight, more ethereal, more radiant, more holy. The outer expression of holiness is always wholeness, and therefore it is very natural that men who regularly withdraw into the high mountain of prayer, even though they never pray for their own health, actually grow more vital and healthy, more holy and whole as the years go by.

"And there was a cloud that over-shadowed them: and a voice came out of the cloud, saying, 'This is my beloved Son: hear Him.'"

This voice was speaking of Jesus. But we must remember that Jesus said, "Ye all have power to become the sons of God." In one breath he said, "I am the light of the world." In another breath he said, "Ye are the light of the world."

Remember the words in Hebrews, that Jesus has made us heirs and co-heirs with Him in the kingdom. And we must not forget, although most of us will never really accept completely, Jesus' words, "Greater works than I have done, shall ye do, because I go to the Father." Therefore, we must realize the fact that whenever any of us step into this "Secret Place of the Most High" and take our stand upon the high mountain of prayer, we make of ourselves "channels" or "sons" with the right to speak God's words through us.

"And suddenly, when they had looked round about, they saw no man any more, save Jesus only with themselves."

No matter how high and how marvelous this experience with God may be, it always comes at last to an end. We cannot live in the mystic cloud of oneness that shuts out the view of the work-a-day world, all day long. It would not be right for us to do so, even though it were possible. When the period of meditation and prayer has run its course it often quite suddenly ends. Suddenly we become aware of our body sitting there, the world comes tumbling back into our consciousness and all the great vision seems to have vanished forever. But have no fear. God abides deep within us, and the power of that hour will accompany us along the way, ready to work miracles upon whomever comes into our presence with faith and love. "They saw Jesus with themselves."

But there is one warning necessary: Power generated in this Quiet Time may be easily dissipated in a way that we least expect. It is so easy, O so very easy, to let idle talk enter in as a reaction after such a time of high spiritual voltage as this is attained. Here we must be on our guard. As we pass the shoemaker's or the barbershop, or meet a kindhearted but gossipy friend, our first impulse is to stop and tell him of the wonderful experience that we had on the mountaintop.

We forget that the one we meet has had no adequate preparation for understanding what we tell. He sees only the
outside of it, not the inside. Could we tarry to hear the
mocking, "O yeah!" or the cynical, "He thinks he has a
private pipe line to God" remark pass from his lips, after
we have gone we never would make such a mistake again.
Jesus, who does not omit a single law of the inner technique
in this "close-up, slow-motion picture" of his method of
helping people, does not fail to make this law clear: "And as
they came down from the mountain, he charged them they
should tell no man what things they had seen."

So much for the experience on the mountaintop. Now we
come to a close-up view of the way this mountaintop vision
manifests itself with miraculous power upon the sick and
ailing in the valley below.

Into this picture now comes an example of one of the
most difficult of all illnesses for prayer to heal. And the situation is rendered doubly difficult because the father of the
sick one already has asked the disciples to heal him, and all
their attempts have failed. So the first fine impulse of faith
has been clouded over with the cold fog of doubt. To make
matters worse, the son has an attack right there as the father
is speaking, "He fell to the ground and wallowed foaming."

Jesus now proceeds to show them a method of spiritual
healing in as perfectly scientific and methodical a way as any
modern psychologist could do. Indeed, in what follows, I
think we shall find the first recorded example of psychoanalysis in history. Jesus here used methods made famous by
Freud and Jung and other great psychologists who "discovered" them two thousand years after Jesus.

First of all, Jesus asked the question, "How long is it ago
since this came unto him?" And the father replied, "Of a

child. And ofttimes it hath cast him into the fire, and into the waters, to destroy him." The value of psychoanalysis was first discovered when a woman suffering from what had been pronounced an incurable disease came to Freud and begged him to let her tell her troubles to him. If she could not be cured, she claimed that it at least gave her peace to tell out her troubles. As she was willing to pay for the time, he finally consented to let her come to him regularly for this outpouring. After a few weeks he discovered that she actually was getting well. Then it was that psychoanalysis became a handmaid to medicine.

So this is a good method to follow in hard cases. I often have asked a person in trouble to tell how it began and when he had finished I would say, "You know when the trouble began, I know when it ends. How fine! Now you can take hold of one end of the log and I'll take hold of the other. What was too heavy for one to handle alone we certainly can handle easily together." "Yes, I know the day and hour when it began," says the other, "but how do you know when it ends?" "It ends right now," I reply.

So we have a little prayer time together in which he gives his end of it; which he is confident that he knows, and I give the end of it which I am confident that I know, into the hands of the Father. And when two "agree together" in this way in giving any trouble or any illness completely into the hands of the Father, He always takes it away.

The next step which Jesus reveals in this "close-up" picture of the complete method of curing the sick is to ask the man to muster all his faith. "If thou canst believe, all things are possible to him that believeth." There is no need of praying where there is no faith. Because Jesus demanded this faith in this case, we know He must have demanded it in all other cases which He cured.

"And straightway the father of the child cried out and said with tears, "I believe." These tears reveal the deep love for this son and the great intensity of his desire for his boy to be well. This love and faith and deep desire is another essential requirement for all prevailing prayer. And the father adds to this also the necessary attribute of absolute honesty. "Help thou mine unbelief." In this final statement he is in effect saying, "I believe, but there is a little area of my mind where I must honestly admit that I find it hard to believe. I have had so many heartbreaks and so many disappointments that there is a little wistful, lingering doubt left. Will you please help me to take that doubt away?"

Occasionally a person comes to me for help and when I ask if he believes, he says, "O yes, I have perfect faith. I am known in my neighborhood for my fine Christian life. I haven't missed going to church for ten years. I offer grace at every meal and say my prayers every night. Of course I believe in prayer." But down in his heart he has great doubts which he is ashamed to reveal lest I shall decline to pray for him if I know how weak his faith really is. The most important thing, almost more important than faith itself, is absolute honesty and absolute humility which leads one to tell frankly his own faults and weaknesses where it would help to effect a cure.

We come now to the next step which was Jesus' rebuking of the foul spirit by saying, "Thou dumb and deaf spirit, I charge thee, come out of him." There is deep and mysterious meaning in this statement that it is well that we don't overlook. The spirit heard him because it obeyed, therefore it was not actually deaf. It cried out so it was not actually dumb. Jesus must have used these words to show that He ascribed no reality to the spirit whatsoever. In other words, he assumed that it was but the shadow of something else,

therefore had no voice or hearing or personality of its own
—and no reality in itself apart from the reality which the
afflicted themselves gave to it.

In my booklet, *The Song of the Souls of Men*, I have described the statement in the Shepherd Psalm, "Yea, though
I walk in the valley of the shadow of death," as really meaning "the nothingness of the nothingness of death." For a
shadow is nothing, and a valley is merely an absence of hills,
a mere hollow space filled with emptiness between two
realities. Certainly the emptiness of the emptiness of death is
nothing to be afraid of. That is all that death ever is when
we come to see it closely. And the demons that haunt us
and throw us down in the fire or in the water, are empty of
voice and empty of hearing and indeed, EMPTY OF
REALITY could we but see them face to face as they
truly are. It was Christ's knowledge of the unreality of sickness, together with His absolute conviction of the ever-
present and all-powerful REALITY OF GOD that enabled
Him to cast out demons and to heal the sick wherever people
came to him in humility, honesty, faith and love.

This epileptic boy had never known Jesus before and had
never learned to love Him. Therefore he was cast in the dust
by the suddenness of the cure. I have discovered that where
there is not sufficient love present in the patient, the cure
is sometimes accompanied with pain or with what is called
"chemicalization." This pain is rarely if ever experienced
where there is love enough present. Jesus now furnished the
love on His part that was sufficient to take the place of what
the other lacked. Tenderly turning to him, "Jesus took him
by the hand, and lifted him up; and he arose."

"And when He was come into the house, His disciples
asked Him privately, 'Why could not we cast him out?' And

He said unto them, 'This kind can come forth by nothing, but by prayer and fasting.' "

"Prayer and fasting" sums up in two words the whole philosophy of healing which I am presenting in this book. Fasting refers to the necessary washing out of the bad and the cleansing through relinquishment of all that would block the way of cure. Prayer refers to the inpouring of power and inspiration through opening oneself to the healing power of God. "Lord empty me of self," is the voice of fasting. "Lord fill me with Thee," is the cry of prayer.

VI. THE WAY I PRAY FOR HEALING

◇◇◇

The Parable of the Sheep on
the Mountain

Once upon a time there was a shepherd who envied a great seer who went up in the mountain to pray, while he, busy with his sheep, had to stay in the valley below.

One day the seer met him and asked, "Why is your face so full of gloom when all the world is full of light?"

"Because, alas, I must stay in the valley with my sheep while you climb to the mountaintop and talk with God."

"Why do you not also climb to the mountaintop?"

"Because I must keep my sheep here where the grass is long and the water in the pool is abundant."

"But the grass up there is also long and the water is much clearer for the sheep than here."

So the shepherd gathered his flock together and led them up the mountain. When he reached the top, there on the tableland, stretched out about him, was truly the finest grass he had ever seen.

"Now at last I can talk to God," he said. But because he did not know the learned words of the seer he could not talk with God. But when his flock was filled and lay down to rest, a great peace came upon him; joy filled his heart, and in this peace and joy all his troubles came to an end.

As he was leading his sheep down the mountain that night, the seer overtook him and asked, "Are you not glad that you took my advice and talked with God on the mountain?"

"Alas," said the shepherd, "after I climbed the mountain, because I am not a learned man, I did not know how to talk with God."

"My friend," said the seer, "do you not know that the sheep you drove up the mountain were your thoughts. And the mountain was prayer. And when your sheep, after their upward climb, rested, and became still, then it was that God came to you and talked with you?"

I HAVE FOUND THAT IT IS NOT THE PRAYER
that creates the miracle, but the condition in consciousness
that the prayer induces. If I can enter a sickroom in the right
state of consciousness and find the patient in the right state
of consciousness, formal prayer of the conventional type is
not always necessary. The Christ is present and the Christ
performs the healing.

What is this healing state of consciousness and how may it
be induced?

The best way to induce it is to live daily practicing the
presence of God.

God is One that cannot be defined. He has to be experienced; light cannot be defined, it also has to be experienced.

The mention of light suggests to me perhaps the simplest
way of explaining the healing process.

Just as the white light of the sun, when viewed through
the prismatic lens, is divided into the primary colors of red,
yellow and blue, so the white light of God, when viewed
through the prism of Prayer, manifests in your life as Faith,
Hope and Love. Indeed, the great secret of perfect health
can be summed up in one sentence: Turn off hate and fear
and self and turn on Faith and Hope and Love, then you
will step instantly into the Secret Place of the Most High
where all healing power abides.

But how can one "turn on" these mighty powers of God?
If such wonderful results will follow, it certainly is worth
our most earnest efforts to find the secret. Let us take them
up one by one.

I. Creative Love

The most powerful of all invisible elements of consciousness is love. The person who lets love flood out from him in all directions, encompassing all persons and all things, both finite and infinite, is doing more to make himself impervious to illness or accident than anything else he could possibly do. The patient on a bed of pain who can release love in this all-encompassing way can be cured. For "God is love; and he that dwelleth in love dwelleth in God, and God in him." (I John 4:16)

But this matter of sending out love everywhere sounds as easy as pushing a button, or turning on a switch, when as a matter of fact it is as colossal an achievement as anything you have ever done. For instance:

1. The first thing you must learn is how to love God. But how can you love an abstraction, which is all that God is to most people? The simplest way ever found of changing God from an abstraction into a reality is by conceiving of Him as a Loving Father, who gives only good gifts to His children.

To love God you will have to believe Him to be the source of all good, and as One who has all power to bring that good to His children. Any belief short of this will very quickly barricade His healing power from you.

This God must be so good and so wise that He would not delegate His power to any worker of evil and mischief, as the devil, and make that delegated power equal to the power He wields Himself. To betray His own children in this fashion would be unworthy of even a human father, much less Almighty God Himself. The power that sin and evil have in the world is the power which we give them by thinking of ourselves as separate from God. Even when we do attempt to creep back to Him it is too often as hirelings rather than as sons. To love God you must think of Him as loving you, and seeking you, and waiting patiently till you turn to Him, a God even more eager to find you and to save you, than you are to find Him. "We love Him because He first loved us." (I John 4:19)

2. You must love all mankind. "If a man says I love God, and hateth his brother, he is a liar: for he that loveth not his brother whom he hath seen, how can he love God whom he hath not seen? and this commandment have we from Him, That he who loveth God love his brother also." (I John 4:20-21) This means that you must let the flood of love that pours through you toward your friends and loved ones be so strong and irresistible and all-encompassing that it can go right on and encompass your enemies as well. If you hate one single man, at that point you hate God, for all men are expressions of God.

If you are praying for someone who is sick, it is of prime importance that you love that person for whom you are praying. To this end and chiefly for this reason, it is very helpful to have the co-operation and sympathy of the friends of the one you pray for. Jesus took the parents of Jairus' daughter with Him when He entered her room, as He wished their love to be joined with His in the momentous act of healing.

3. You should love the very ailment you have come to cure. The moment that a person loves a thing and ceases to fear it, he has power to command it. Great animal tamers know that, and great sickness tamers soon find it out. Otherwise they cease to be great sickness tamers. Physicians who have no fear of disease not only become immune to it themselves, but they soon bring immunity to others.

Learn to look upon the illness which you are trying to banish, lovingly and patiently. Study it carefully to find what it is that it is supposed to be cleansing away. Look upon it as a mother looks upon soap and water which she wishes to apply to the dirty neck and ears of her boy. The chances are he will squirm and squeal and moan and groan; and, when asked if he wants to remain dirty and catch the small-pox, he may say that he'd rather have smallpox than soap and water in the strong, relentless hands of a vigorous, loving mother. But when the boy learns to trust his mother and to love soap and water, it will take him actually less time to get clean than when he feared and fought them.

The first important basic principle that should guide you when going into a sickroom is to go with a friendly, loving attitude toward every person and everything, and above all, with a friendly, fearless attitude toward the sickness itself.

The snake charmers of India and Africa find the venom of the most deadly snakes has no power to hurt them if they have no fear in their hearts and only loving thoughts toward the snakes. You, yourself, may have experienced how quickly nervous, dangerous watchdogs that rush upon you, change their growls and yelps into fawning and tail wagging when they are persuaded that you neither fear nor hate them. Jesus has told us that when we turn the other cheek with peace and love in our hearts we will turn even our enemies into friends.

Now it may seem a strange stretching of Jesus' statement, "With what measure ye mete it shall be measured unto you," to apply it to dangerous or even fatal illnesses, but let me assure you that the principle really works. I might say very frankly that the more seemingly conscious and intelligent a foe is, the slower he is to respond to this subtle inner law that transforms him into a friend. A human enemy won't at first believe you love him when you turn the other cheek. He will judge you by *his* own worst motives and imagine that you are trying to trick him. An animal will accept your love more quickly and trustingly. Nonresistant, subconscious matter, as disease germs, will be rendered harmless still more quickly. Perhaps this is why jolly, fun-loving doctors are more effective than the overly-serious kind. It certainly is true that fearless, calm and loving doctors are far more effective than the timorous kind who hate and fear the disease with which they are engaging battle. If you don't believe calm and fearless loving will kill disease germs, or any evil, just try it.

Now, in a very practical analysis, let me prove that disease is much more benevolent and loving an instrument than most people realize. I shall begin with a true story taken from the first World War. A man had been severely wounded and blood poisoning had set in. The lack of disinfectants and hospital supplies made it impossible to take care of his infected arm. When he finally reached the base hospital and the dirty dressings were taken away, to the amazement of the young doctor assigned to the case, the wound was already overrun with maggots. In deep consternation and afraid that the case was hopeless, he asked a more experienced physician how they could get rid of the vermin, and if there was any hope. The senior physician immediately brightened. "I thought he was a gonner, but now I know that he will get well. Bind up his arm again and for God's sake don't remove the maggots. They are going after the germs and will save him from systemic blood poisoning. It's the luckiest thing that possibly could have happened to him." The man recovered. The maggots had done their work.

It seems terrible to love maggots, but in this instance they were doing what no one else could do, because they were willing to devour, not the healthy flesh, but the poisons of the dead tissue, which otherwise would have taken the life of the man.

This sounds almost as gruesome as the incident in the "Rhyme of the Ancient Mariner" where the sailor, upon whom a curse had been hung because of his wantonly killing of an albatross, finally turned his gaze upon the slimy, crawling things upon the stagnant sea and "blessed them unaware." That moment his curse was lifted.

Look lovingly upon asthma, a little maggot that is trying to eat out—not your life—but the blood poison of self-pity. Look at the germ of rheumatism as a little "crawling thing" that is trying to help you by eating out the blood poison of criticism and cynicism. Look upon these illnesses as soap and water being applied by a loving Father to wash away other things that He knows are more important than the illness itself.

But just because soap and water is good, is not any reason why one should go around the town with his face constantly lathered up. I can never forget seeing the fire wagon dashing down the street one day with the driver who had rushed from the barber's chair at the sound of the gong, sitting in the driver's seat, with one cheek nicely shaved and the other all lathered with shaving soap. A person afflicted with a stubborn, chronic illness is merely a fireman dashing about his daily work with soap still on his cheek.

As the little boy should help his mother wash his ears if he wishes to get the ordeal over more quickly, and as the fireman should not have debated politics so long with the barber, so if we will get rid of our besetting sin of wrong thinking, we will the sooner get rid of the embarrassment of the soap that the world calls sickness.

II. CREATIVE FAITH

One cannot have creative faith if he has fear, for fear is the most destructive faith there is. Fear is faith that the powers of evil are greater than the powers of good. But Creative Love, as I have described it, will take care of that. "Perfect love casteth out fear." How can you fear when you love a God who is all-loving toward you; how can you fear when you love all mankind? How can you fear when you love all that God has created, even the very illness which you are asking God to remove. When you love God, when you love all men, when you love all things—even germs and maggots—there is absolutely nothing that you will find it possible for you to fear. In the calm which such an all-encompassing love begets in you, all power is yours.

III. CREATIVE PEACE

Out of the union of Creative Love and of Creative Faith is born Creative Peace, the greatest miracle-producing power known to man. For Peace—not the peace "that the world giveth," but "the Peace that passeth all understanding"— clears the channel and makes the way straight for the Power of God to manifest in its completest form. "Our cargoes," says a writer, "only come to us over calm seas."

The actual process of removing the illness, then, consists of releasing, first Love, then Faith, then Peace upon the thing to be removed. Taking one's stand upon this firm foundation of Peace which this Love and Faith have created in you, all you need to do is to turn quietly to the illness and either

1. Deny it away or
2. Laugh it away or
3. Relinquish it away or
4. Know it away.

I. THE DENIAL METHOD

"The maid is *not dead*, but sleepeth!" said Jesus.

The denial method consists of denying the seeming badness with one quick, sharp denial, and then following it up with a number of strong, vigorous affirmations of good.

My first experiment in the field of effective prayer was with this method. I based it upon Jesus' statement that the Kingdom of Heaven is within us. Using that as my starting point I would say emphatically and aloud, "There is no sickness in heaven. All is harmony, wholeness and health." Discovering fear to be the chief obstacle to Creative Faith, I found the following prayer very effective: "Our Heavenly Father, I know that I, made in Thy likeness and image, know no fear, for, being in Christ, and being the knowledge and consciousness of Thee, I know only Thee, that Thou art the God of Love, giver of every perfect gift, and when I abide in Thee and rest eternally in Thy Holy Love, nothing evil can then reach me without first passing through Thee, being transformed in the process into perfect harmony, perfect wholeness, and perfect love."

To have a few such denials and affirmations memorized and ready for instant use, especially for those who are awakened in the middle of the night with recurrent attacks of different forms of ailments, can prove a great comfort, as anyone who has tried it well knows.

The practical way to use this method would be to deny the material cause and affirm the spiritual cleansing first and then apply it directly to the illness. For instance, in anemia one could assert, "There is no unhappiness nor weariness in Heaven; all life in Heaven is buoyant, fresh, happy, and joyful; there is no retarding of the joy that flows through the channels of consciousness, all is joyous, free and over-flowing with gladness, bringing perfect health, perfect harmony, perfect wholeness."

For stomach ulcers: "There is no sense of inadequacy in heaven, everyone has complete understanding, absolute effi-ciency, everything is done with perfect ease and one's ideas come in perfect sequence and order, just the right ideas at the right time to meet every problem and every situation in which one is placed."

For heart trouble: "There is no discord nor misunder-standing nor withdrawal of love in heaven, there is nothing but perfect harmony and perfect love flowing in perfect rhythm and perfect ease to every part of one's being through all time and through all eternity, bringing perfect harmony, perfect health, perfect wholeness."

This is no place to insist upon the highest tests of classical English which says that one should never use two words where one will do. Tautology, repetition of the same word, or better still of different words that are exact synonyms, like "wholeness" and "health," is a good thing, in the "knock method," as the purpose is to drum the realization into one's subconscious mind. There is no need to drum it into God's mind, or into the mind of your own soul. For God knows it and your own soul knows it, but your mind, especially your own subconscious mind with all its negative records which it has been faithfully keeping of all past fears and doubts and sins through many years, has to be hammered back into normalcy. The subconscious mind is the old reprobate that has to be "converted."

Although advanced souls who have learned the art of living constantly in the consciousness of the presence of God very rarely use the denial and affirmation method, I still think it is one of the best of all known methods for the beginner. Jesus said, "Ask and it shall be given you; seek and ye shall find; knock, and it shall be opened unto you." (Luke 11:19) I think of the petitionary prayer as the "ask method," and this denial method as the "knock method." And I have found, ever since my first baby came, that a little child with a spoon in one hand and an empty bowl in the other, before he graduates to the more polite and orthodox "asking method," usually makes his needs heard by the "knocking method." Why can't we, too, begin as a little child?

II. The Laughing Method

I had one habit in the use of English, when I was a schoolboy, of saying, "I will lay down" instead of "I will lie down." Teachers tried their best with red ink and blue pencil to correct this fault in my compositions, all to no avail. Then one day I used the expression in the presence of a classmate who knew I was planning to teach English some day, and he laughed loud and long. He held his sides and laughed "fit to split." When I finally calmed him down long enough to make him tell me what he was laughing at, I was so mortified that this bad habit leaped out of the upper window of my brain and never dared show its face again.

Remembering this experience I thought I would try it on sickness. So one day when my three-year-old daughter had a terrible earache that no treatment seemed competent to ease, I went to her room, shut myself in alone with her, and seeing her, in my imagination, crying, not at the earache but at a shadow of our neighbor's house on the lawn, I pretended that she was interpreting the shadow as the house fallen down. Concentrating my mind on the absurdity of mistaking a shadow of a house for the house itself, and the equal absurdity of mistaking an earache, which, as seen in heaven, is a mere shadow of Reality, I began to laugh. I laughed as my student friend had laughed at me, I laughed loud and long. When my little girl looked at me in wonder, I held my sides and laughed all the more. When she started to cry again I drowned out her sobs by laughing "fit to split." She gave me one open-eyed stare of bewilderment and immediately went to sleep. When she awoke again she began to cry again, and my wife said that she would go to her this time as I had been so good as to look after her before. But my wife immediately called down, "She says she wants you to come, because, she says, you make the earache go away." So I went up, drove my wife from the room, closed the door, and sat down and resumed my laughter. In three minutes the pain was entirely gone again and she was sound asleep. And the earache never returned. Indeed, twenty years have passed since then, and yet she has had no earache. Just as my bad grammar in the presence of laughter and ridicule, it "never dared show its face again."

You have often seen doctors laugh away little, trivial illnesses, especially cases of nerves or of pure imagination, but the laughter I am speaking about, and which I have used, is spiritual creative laughter, laughter that is heard in heaven. It is the heaven-born laughter based upon the firm foundation of a peace that passeth all understanding, under-girded with heavenly love and heavenly faith. If it seems too severe to try it on your friends, try it on yourself some day. You may be in for a surprise. Perhaps your wife will laugh with you.

III. The Relinquishing Method

It may seem strange to say that we can get a thing by giving it away, but is not that the law of the tides? Is it not the law of love? "With what measure ye mete it shall be measured unto you." (Mark 4:24) "Give and it shall be given unto you." (Luke 6:38)

And what greater proof of complete love and complete trust in a loving Father can be expressed than by utterly re-linquishing oneself or one's friends to be taken into the Kingdom or continued in his illness IF IT BE GOD'S WILL?

When Hawthorne's daughter, Una, came down in Rome with the dreaded Italian fever, the mother was alone with her. When the doctors gave up hope, she felt a great bit-terness and rebellion against God who would take this favorite child of Nathaniel's while he was away, knowing how her death would crush him. For hours this spirit of re-bellion and bitterness filled her, but finally, after several days when she knew death was near, she aroused herself and said, "If she must die, at least I shall have the privilege of giving her to the Father." So she carried her to the window and gave her to the Father to do with as He knew best; then she put her in her crib, and left the room. In a few minutes the nurse called her excitedly. The face of the child had suddenly taken on new color. The pallor of death was disappearing. The doctors were summoned, not to find a dead girl, but a quickly recovering one.

A minister once told me that he had only one example of truly answered prayer in his entire ministry. He told me how he had gone to the home of a family where the little child was not expected to live. It was in a small town, and he lived across the alley, so he entered the back door without stopping to knock. He found the parents weeping in the living room. They told him that just as he came through the back door, the doctor had left by the front door, after saying that it was now only a matter of a few hours before the child would die. The minister said, "Let us pray together then that if it is the Father's will to take him, you will abide by His will, but if He will let him return to health, you will solemnly dedicate him and yourselves to God to see that he grows into an unselfish, God-fearing man." So they all knelt down and prayed, with emphasis upon relinquishing the child, and not on keeping him.

"And that," said the minister, "is the only time my prayer was answered."

And that, we may add, is probably the only time that he and those he prayed with had completely released the loved one wholly into the hands of the Father.

I was once asked to pray for a little Catholic boy who had spinal meningitis. The parents pressed down so hard for his recovery and were so brokenhearted at the thought of losing him that I found my prayers were "hitting the ceiling," the "ceiling" the parents' own wills were creating. Finally a sister called me up and said, "He is barely breathing this morning. The priest has administered Extreme Unction."

"Then they have completely given him up at last?"

"Yes. They are reconciled to God's will and will give him to the Father."

"Good," I replied, "then we can roll up our sleeves and start to work." Instantly our prayers began to go clear through to the throne of God. And the little child was fully restored to health in a few days.

IV. THE KNOWING METHOD

This is the most powerful of all methods of sending sickness into oblivion. It was the method Jesus used. It goes far beyond denials, it goes far beyond laughter. It has nothing to deny, and nothing to laugh away. It is based upon clear understanding, positive conviction regarding all the facts and principles involved. Where there is absolute faith on the part of the one praying, absolute faith on the part of the one prayed for, and absolute justice and right in the thing prayed about, this Knowing Method functions with wonderful power.

Jeremiah *knew* that Sennacherib's army would not take Jerusalem because Sennacherib had broken his sacred covenant that he would not attack the city.

Paul *knew* that the sailors and the passengers aboard the storm-tossed ship would not be destroyed in the threatened shipwreck because he had received absolute assurance from God that he would reach Rome.

Jesus *knew* that the man sick of the palsy would be cured because his faith and that of his four friends had been so great that they had opened the roof to let him down in His presence.

Jesus *knew* that the servant would get well when he heard the Centurion's statement that all Jesus needed to do was to speak the word and his servant would recover.

Jesus *knew* that the Syro-Phoenician woman's daughter would be healed when she expressed such great humility that she would be willing to "eat the crumbs" at the Master's table.

Such knowing faith is something to be sought for, not something to be achieved without effort and sacrifice. It requires the making of one's feet into hind's feet, of making the conscious and the subconscious mind co-operate as a unit in perfect understanding and positive acceptance of the great basic principles of life.

The conditions are most perfect for its achievement when there is perfect love, perfect faith, and perfect peace, combined in perfect orchestration. The most signal failure to meet this perfect orchestration in the story of Jesus was when he returned to Nazareth, "and there could do no mighty work because of their unbelief." The most perfect example of this perfect orchestration outside of Jesus' life was the experience at Pentecost where one hundred and twenty souls came together "in one place and of one mind." In modern times some of the best examples of such *knowing* faith are to be found in the lives of George Müller and George Washington Carver. The best examples of this perfect inner orchestration that have come under my observation I have described in the Twelve Parable Miracles of Answered Prayer which are in the final chapter of *I Will Lift Up Mine Eyes*. I shall quote one of these here:

The Parable of the Light That Shone in the Darkness

One day a man received a letter. And this is what the letter said:

"Because something you said helped me to see the light and because it brought me great comfort when trouble was thick upon me, I am coming to you again for help. This time my little daughter, my only child, is attacked by illness which the doctors say will prove fatal. In my anxiety and despair, I am turning to you for help. I trust all to your prayer."

For a little while this letter troubled the man. Here was

one leaning upon him for something he knew he could not give. Nevertheless, knowing that the need was great, he sat down and wrote the man as follows:

"Step off the top of a ten-story building and give yourself without question to the air, knowing that the parachute will open and save you. As the air is all about you and is sufficient to support the parachute, so God's love is all about you and is sufficient to support my prayer. I shall pray for you. Love will be in my prayer. Step into the atmosphere of Divine Love and give yourself unresistingly to its power."

As he wrote and even as the carrier went off with his letter, the man ceased to think of the stranger who had written him, but thought rather of the infinite trust which could fill a man's soul, that could make him write for help as this one had done; and as he thought, the one who had written faded out of sight and nothing but light remained, the clear, bright light of trust, and then he knew that trust was one of the greatest things in the universe. For trust is something which no manner of evil can hurt, it is just like the air: when the sword cleaves it, it gathers together again; when one would destroy it, he finds it cannot be touched. Trust cannot be exhausted, for the more it is used, the stronger it grows; and the more it is reviled the more impervious and indestructible it becomes. No impurities or weaknesses can find lodgement in trust any more than darkness can find a foothold in light. When light enters a room, darkness runs out of the door. When trust fills a man, evils flee from his being—yes, out through his very pores. Trust is impenetrable by anything which is unlike itself, just as light is impenetrable by darkness. It is impervious to all thrusts of those who would destroy it, and yet it enslaves and binds and limits no man who surrenders himself captive unto it.

Thus the petitioning friend faded out of the man's vision and in his place he saw only trust. Where he stood all shadows of darkness had vanished and there was only light.

And thus having written and thus having sat and thought awhile the man was interrupted by pressing demands and went away and forgot the matter entirely. A few days later a letter came from the troubled one saying that his daughter had miraculously become sound and well at that very hour, that other beautiful blessings had come into his home, that his business had commenced to prosper, and that his God had begun to do his thinking for him.

Then it was that a great wonder came to the man, for experiences like this were at that time new to him. "Is escape from the evils that beset us as simple as that?" he asked. "Can a man be made whole by his faith alone? Can all darkness vanish from a room by the simple act of turning on the light?"

But some of my readers may say that all this requires some mystic or metaphysical capacities which many do not possess. How can a man of action, who has little mystic sense, have a faith that can move mountains?

Such a person should be set at work doing something. That is where diagnosing a specific cause for each illness, according to Chapter IV, actually helps. Set the patient to work overcoming that particular fault that has helped bring on the sickness. That gives him something to DO and as he overcomes the cause and *knows* that he is overcoming it, he gets a deep, inner conviction of achievement which furnishes him the practical basis for KNOWING that God will make him well. So while you pray for him, and *he works* at overcoming his "sins," the two—faith and works—go hand in hand toward a merry cure.

VII. EXAMPLES OF ANSWERED PRAYER

◇◇◇

The Parable of the Wrestler
for the Lord

One day a man who had been trained as a wrestler found himself face to face with Death. "I have met some mighty foes," he thought to himself. "But this one looks like the toughest and strongest of them all. I shall need every ounce of strength and every bit of skill that I ever possessed."

Now the man knew that the first thing necessary for a wrestler is to be unafraid of his antagonist. He knew from experience, also, that when your foe is greater than you, you must not throw him, you must let him throw himself.

So, unafraid, he awaited, yea, even welcomed the onrush of the enemy. Then as the adversary bore down upon him, he stepped aside. The place where he stood before found him absent, invisible, and Death stumbling over his own feet fell prostrate.

And so, having learned the art of wrestling with Death, he gave up wrestling against mere adversaries of flesh and blood and went forth to wrestle against forces of Evil, against Sin, Sickness, and Death as they bore down upon his friends.

To mothers who came to him saying, "My child is

dying," he quietly replied, "Have no fear. Give your child into the protecting arms of the Father who is in Heaven. Let the kind Father take him, and keep him, if it is His Will. Do not fight, do not struggle. Accept with radiant acquiescence whatever the Father decides. Let Death come on if he wishes to. He cannot touch anyone who is completely given into the Father's arms, unless his time has come according to the Father's Will."

And Death came rushing on time after time to fall headlong without securing his prey, because where the child had been he now was not, having been given so completely into the protecting arms of the Father of Infinite Love.

And so the man ceased to be known as a wrestler for this team or that team, and became known as a Wrestler for the Lord.

IN THE SUMMER OF 1937 I WAS SHARING WITH Dr. William Adams Brown, in leading a spiritual retreat on church unity at Adelynrood, South Byfield, Massachusetts. One morning when I had finished my talk, I was introduced to Dr. Loring T. Swaim, nationally known specialist in rheumatism and arthritis, who, with his wife, had made a special trip from their home in Boston to see me. At that time he was Secretary of the American Rheumatism Association.

This is the story he had to tell:

"Ten years ago I became conscious of real need in my own life. I was spiritually starved, so I went into the woods to try to think out a plan. I took your book, *The Soul's Sincere Desire*, in an effort to learn to pray, if possible. I learned a great deal about myself and I learned much about the technique of prayer from the book. Several years later, having met the Oxford Group, I began the practice of two-way prayer, which is listening to God.

"I never start a day's work now without a Quiet Time and prayer with my wife. When problems arise in the office, my assistants pray about them. We allow no misunderstanding to develop between us because we try to be wholly honest with each other. We ask God for a united policy for our office. A young Episcopal woman, a member of the Companionship at Adelynrood, helps me to straighten out the emotional and spiritual problems of my patients, as they are willing to apply spiritual laws to their lives. We have discovered that there is a close correlation between the mental and spiritual attitudes and the ups and downs in arthritis.

Casting out fears and resentments and trusting oneself completely to God's care almost invariably bring about a noticeable decrease in the symptoms and an improvement in the arthritis.

"I was asked to read a paper on 'Studies in the Control of the Psychogenic Factors in Chronic Rheumatoid Arthritis' at an International Meeting of Physicians in London. I decided I would reveal to them something about the nature of my spiritual approach to this field. The paper was splendidly received and several physicians told me that they had had similar experiences in their practices, through the development of a trust in God."

If all physicians would follow similar methods I have no doubt that the proportion of cures, especially in all the very stubborn and difficult types of illness, would greatly increase. As a matter of fact most physicians do follow these methods more or less, but do it unostentatiously, and many of them, unconsciously. A great number of eminent physicians such as those at the Mayo Clinic at Rochester, are unselfish men, clear of nearly all the major sins themselves. "They *all* have faith," as one doctor said, "for if they do not have faith in God, they at least have faith in the healing power of nature." But to use this method effectively and consistently, one should do as Dr. Swaim does—definitely clean out the channels before the day begins, and then turn to God, or to one's highest conception of God, and give Him the praise and the glory.

The kingdom of Heaven, as I have found it, is a state of consciousness that so transcends the ordinary state of consciousness that afflicts us and plagues us on this earthly plane, that, when properly experienced it literally sweeps away most of the limitations that flesh is heir to.

I use all the methods for attaining this consciousness described by Jesus, as far as I am able. I ask, I seek, I knock, but in the moments of crisis I frequently resort to the last one. The method of *"Knock and it shall be opened to you"* as I have experienced it, and as I would recommend it to others, can be summed up as follows:

First, clear out anything that blocks, or separates you from your sense of oneness with God. An effective way to do that is to turn in thought to God and Heaven, or to your highest conception of God and Heaven, deny the existence in Heaven of the wrong thing thought or felt, and then realize that in God and Heaven the opposite condition prevails. One must dismiss completely from his mind the thought that the wrong thing felt or seen is permanent, and then follow instantly with the realization that the opposite condition exists here and now.

One of the first opportunities of testing this method, which I had, was in the spring of 1926. I went to the college one day and heard the dean announcing that an automobile carrying four of our college students had turned turtle three times, and that little "Margaret" would not live through the day. I instantly recalled that "Margaret" was one of a group of students who had made a practice of coming to my house every Tuesday evening to listen to a brief talk which they had asked me to give on "Living in the Kingdom here and now." One day my wife asked me to see Margaret, because she had a spiritual face, and a wistful look which rather touched her.

So I had asked Margaret to come and see me, as I wanted to talk to her. She replied instantly "Oh, I want to. I will come and see you soon."

And now she would never see me. She would not keep her promise.

But why shouldn't she? When we had spoken to each

other it had been on an unselfish plane, a mere desire on my part, and that of my wife, to help her; and a sincere desire on her part to receive more spiritual help from me. Yes, it had been on an unselfish plane—and what is an unselfish plane but a HEAVENLY PLANE?

I hopped into my car and hurried to the hospital.

When I arrived I found the president of the college and his wife, and eight members of the faculty in the hall outside the bedroom. Within the room I could see the little unconscious figure, and at the bedside sat her widowed mother, who had come from another city during the night, to be with her in her closing hours.

I entered, and was introduced to the mother who immediately went out and closing the door left me all alone. Two doctors came in and they also closed the door, but neither of them seemed to mind my being there. I might have been an invisible angel from heaven the way people treated me. And then it suddenly dawned upon me that the mother hoped that I could help her daughter through prayer. I felt very humble, and for a moment very shaky. And then I turned away from myself and the little mundane world about me, and put my trust in God and Heaven, and held fast, with all the strength that I had, to the great immutable promises of God.

I asked the doctors what they were doing with the little body which they were handling rather roughly.

"We are trying to find out whether or not she will be paralyzed for life if she does get well."

"Do you think there is any hope for her recovery?"

"We don't see how there can be. When she was picked up there was no blood pressure, no heart beat, no breathing. We do not know how long she had been in that condition."

I spoke no more to them. While they went steadily about

their task I went about mine. We might have been in two totally different worlds.

"I asked her to come and see me," I thought to myself, "and in that request there lay no desire for fame, or glory, or money, or selfish reward of any kind—that request was prompted by pure unselfish Love. Love is the greatest power in the Universe. A request of Love is like a command of God —it is regal, kingly and brooks no disobedience. I believe that little girl will obey that command, I believe that she will keep her promise, and come and see me."

Then I looked at the table where stood a vase filled with flowers. It flashed upon me how much the vase typified little Margaret—beautiful—delicate—fragile. I knew that if such a vase were to fall from the table, and we should take a moving picture of it, all we would need to do would be to turn the picture backward, and instead of seeing the vase crashing *downward* into fragments and destruction, we would see the fragments drawn UPWARD into wholeness and life.

I saw then that all life is similar to a series of moving pictures in the hands of God. If we let God do *all* of the turning, the movement would *always* be UPWARD toward life, toward Love, toward Heaven. But because we insist on doing most of the turning, with our little selfish and ignorant desires, most of the movement of life is downward toward destruction, toward misery and death.

Then instantly I said to myself:

"What is the stronger force in this universe, the force of gravity and selfishness and death, or the force of God—of wholeness and Love?" With sincere faith and positive conviction I said to myself "*I put my faith in God and Love.*"

And to the amazement of all, and to the joy of her mother,

and all of her friends, within a few months she made a complete recovery.

Another time came when my own two beautiful daughters, one fourteen and one twelve, had been ill with scarlet fever for three weeks, when suddenly instead of taking a turn for the better conditions took a turn for the worse. Their throats closed until the tiny opening would not admit a single drop of water, and scarcely permitted breathing in safety. The doctor phoned for an ambulance and said to us, "I lost a patient whose condition was much less serious than this, just last week."

After the ambulance had left, the two nurses we had engaged were both sobbing—one was a Catholic and one was a Christian Scientist—never expecting to see the little girls again. My wife and I went into an upper room, put our arms around each other and had a brief period of prayer.

"You have often told others that they must relinquish their children to the Father," my wife said. "Now is the time when we must relinquish our little girls. If it is God's Plan for them to go, rather than that they should be crippled, or weakened all their lives from this illness, I would be willing that God should take them."

"I too, would prefer to see them taken than to be returned to us if it is against the Plan of the Father," I replied.

"God may want them for the Kingdom of Heaven," she added, "and of course we know that we alone would suffer —for to them it would be a great and glorious experience."

"I have just this one prayer to offer for their recovery," I said, "and it is this: That if they are to enter the Kingdom, we here shall highly resolve and devoutly promise the Father that we shall try to make our own home as completely an expression of the Kingdom of Heaven on earth, a place of love and harmony, and service and comfort for others—as we are able to make it. Then, if God wishes them to abide in the Kingdom He may let them abide in our home instead."

When a few weeks later the little girls were restored to us, with no after effects of the illness at all, completely recovered, their eyes seemed to shine with the light of heaven within them.

Another experience was the following:

One Sunday morning I received a telephone call. It was from Mrs. Simpson, one of my dearest friends in Minneapolis. She said, "Can I see you this morning regarding something that is of great importance to my life—it is something that cannot be put off, as I am leaving for the Mayo Hospital tomorrow."

I replied that I could see her after my morning Bible Class at Plymouth Church. But little was I prepared for the unusual story that I was to hear.

"Last Wednesday morning," she began, when we were alone together, "I received a telephone call from Miss Stella Holbrook one of my closest friends. Her voice betrayed great excitement, and I could see that she was under a great strain. She said, 'My dearest friend is in deadly peril. I must see you immediately. Will you come to see me, or shall I go to you?' I asked if she would come to me.

"In a few moments she arrived at my apartment. She looked haggard, and as she staggered to a chair and sat down she looked me searchingly in the face. 'The one who is in deadly peril,' she said, 'is yourself.'

" 'What!' I exclaimed, 'Why I have not been sick for years, and I never felt better in my life than I do this moment.'

" 'No matter,' she said, 'you must see a doctor at once.'

" 'Explain yourself,' I said.

" 'You must listen to me, even if what I say may seem absurd. I had a dream about you last night. I could see you walking up and down the room holding your head between your hands. Finally you turned toward me so that I saw your face, and I could see that you had gone insane. It made such a deep impression upon me that I couldn't sleep. I walked the floor all night.'

" 'What!' I exclaimed, 'This sounds absurd!'

" 'No matter how it sounds,' she replied, 'You must see a doctor, if only for my own peace of mind. I never had a dream that was so real. Promise me that you will go to a physician at once.'

"So I promised and went. To my surprise the doctor discovered that I had a tumor that might press upon my brain and cause insanity unless something was done about it right away. He said that I should be operated upon at once. He advised me not to wait twenty-four hours. I told him that I wanted to have Rochester check upon me first. So I am starting to Rochester tomorrow morning—but I wanted to talk with you first, and have your prayers joined with mine."

"To pray for a situation of this kind," I began, "and to pray with faith, requires that we first clear the ground. Anything associated with divination of any kind crushes one down under the sense of doom. It makes one feel helpless. First of all we must understand that there is no power in the psychic realm—and that is the realm where divination resides—that can stand against the far greater power that functions in the spiritual or the heavenly realm. To foresee a thing in time, is just like foreseeing a thing in space. If you saw a bridge down in front of you in space, you would not run head on into it, would you? You would make a detour around it. Well, it is the same way in time. Miss Holbrook, being as close to you in spirit as your own guardian angel, was able to climb the high hill of Love and see a bridge down, as it were, out there in time. She foresaw an illness that you seemed to be running into head-on. But that will not be necessary. You can make a detour around it."

"And how can I do that?" she asked, just as naturally as she would ask the way to Des Moines. She was a remarkable woman, and I never saw greater poise and calm.

"Just as you would make a detour around a danger in space," I replied, "Turn to the right. And by *right* I mean just exactly what Jesus meant when He said to Peter after he had been fishing all night without success, 'Cast out your net on the right side!' The right side is always God's side. In other words turn to God. Turn to Him completely and utterly, and put your entire problem into His hands with complete faith that He has the power to remove the danger from you."

"I understand, exactly," she replied. "You know that I have no fear for myself. I have never worried about myself, so you can count on me not to block your prayer in any way. Moreover, I can arrange my summer so that I can go off to the mountains and spend the entire summer in happy work and quiet prayer."

"Splendid," I replied, "Now I feel sure that God will take care of you."

Three and one half months later I received another telephone call. "I am back from my summer vacation," came the voice, "and I want to invite you and Mrs. Clark to take dinner with me next Tuesday evening at the Women's Club here in Minneapolis."

On the beautiful veranda overlooking Loring Park, the

most beautiful view one can obtain in the very heart of Minneapolis, Mrs. Clark and I sat down with her before a lovely autumn repast, looked at a beautiful autumn sunset, and listened to her remarkable story.

"Well, I went to the Mayo Clinic," she began. "They verified exactly what the doctor up here had said. The surgeon in charge advised immediate operation. I wrote my friends to come down, and was making all preparations when the doctor said that he wanted Dr. Judd and Dr. Will Mayo to examine me. 'Dr. Will Mayo,' he said, 'has something greater than the power of the average diagnostician. He has *intuition* —one might call it spiritual *insight*.' When Dr. Mayo examined me he verified what the other two doctors had already discovered, but Dr. Will Mayo, as though speaking from a sixth sense, said, 'Don't operate right away. Go away for three months, and then come back, and we will decide what to do.'

"So I went away to the mountains. I spent the time literally and figuratively in the mountains of prayer. I had no fears, in fact I gave no thought whatever to this trouble, but turned my thought to God and my fellow man. Then when September came I went back to the hospital.

"When the specialist had finished his X-ray examination he exclaimed, 'Something must be wrong here. I must have Dr. Judd check up on this at once. What would people think of the Mayo Clinic if it had on its records that you had a growth the size of a hen's egg, in June, and that it had completely vanished by September!' So Dr. Judd examined me, and when he got through he seized both of my hands, jumped up and down and exclaimed, 'This is a miracle!' "

The Mayo Clinic is recognized all over the world as an institution where records are carefully kept, and its findings are accepted as authoritative. Another institution that holds the respect of scientists all over the world is the Rockefeller Medical Foundation. Let me close this chapter with the words of my friend, Dr. Alexis Carrel, Member Emeritus of the Foundation. In his fascinating book *Man, the Unknown*, he expresses in no uncertain terms his profound conviction regarding the power and value of this spiritual approach.

In all countries, at all times, people have believed in the existence of miracles in the more or less rapid healing of the sick at places of pilgrimage, at certain sanctuaries. But after the great impetus of science during the nineteenth century, such belief completely disappeared. It was generally admitted, not only that miracles did not exist, but that they could not exist. As the laws of thermodynamics make perpetual motion impossible, so physiological laws oppose miracles. Such is still the attitude of most physiologists and physicians. However, in view of the facts observed during the last fifty years this attitude cannot be sustained. The most important cases of miraculous healing have been recorded by the Medical Bureau of Lourdes. Our present conception of the influence of prayer upon pathological lesions is based upon the observation of patients who have been cured almost instantaneously of various affections, such as peritoneal tuberculosis, cold abscesses, osteitis, suppurating wounds, lupus, cancer, etc. The process of healing changes little from one individual and another. Often, an acute pain. Then a sudden sensation of being cured. In a few seconds, a few minutes, at the most a few hours, wounds are cicatrized, pathological symptoms disappear, appetite returns. Sometimes functional disorders vanish before the anatomical lesions are repaired. The skeletal deformations of Pott's Disease, the cancerous glands, may still persist two or three days after the healing of the main lesions. The miracle is chiefly characterized by an extreme acceleration of the processes of organic repair. There is no doubt that the rate of cicatrization of the anatomical defects is much greater than the normal one. The only condition indispensable to the occurrence of the phenomenon is prayer. But there is no need for the patient himself to pray, or even to have any religious faith. It is sufficient that someone around him be in the state of prayer. Such facts are of profound significance. They show the reality of certain relations, of still unknown nature, between psychological and organic processes. They prove the objective importance of the spiritual activities, which hygienists, physicians, educators and sociologists have almost neglected to study. They open to man a new world.

VIII. THE RIVER OF HEALING

<figure>◇◇</figure>

The Parable of the Radio in the Secret Place

There was a man who regularly tuned in to the radio. Every morning and every evening he listened to the news broadcasts of this world. Politics, wars, murders, fires, scandals, filled his day and filled his night. At times he wondered how he could carry it all and not break under it. One day he met a minister who always carried such peace and sweetness in his soul that merely to look into his face made one's day more filled with light. One day he asked the minister what he did to get that way.

"I tune in morning and night."

"I too, tune in to the radio morning and night," said the other, "but it doesn't do that to me."

"Perhaps you don't use the same kind of radio I use."

"Nonsense," said the man. "You don't mean to tell me that a mere difference in shape, style, or make of radio can make all that difference. My radio is shaped like a table, for instance. What is yours shaped like?"

"Mine is shaped like a book," said the minister. "In fact, I carry it always with me—in my pocket."

"*A pocket radio!*" *exclaimed the man. "Let me see it!"*

The minister drew forth a little testament containing the gospels and psalms. "God is always speaking to man," he went on. "His broadcasting station is going night and day, sending love, peace, joy, guidance, all the time. Fortunately for us, some great souls in the past who were sufficiently in tune to hear His voice have made transcriptions of His words, and recorded them in forms that may be handed down through the ages. So that is why I carry this with me. It is like a transcription of the voice of God Himself."

So the man went his way, and from that time forth he took pains not to spend his time tuning in to wars and rumors of wars. He tuned in to the receiving set shaped like a book. And out of it he found that there came flowing a constant stream of inspired Truth that brought healing to any situation into which he was cast.

"And he carried me way in the Spirit to a mountain great and high, and showed me the holy city Jerusalem, coming down out of heaven from God, having the glory of God: . . . And I saw no temple therein: for the Lord God Almighty is the temple thereof. And the city hath no need for the sun, neither for the moon, to shine upon it, for the glory of God lightens it. . . .

"And he showed me, in the midst of the streets of the city, a river of the Water of Life, clear as crystal, proceeding out of the throne of God. And on this side of the river and on that was the Tree of Life, bearing twelve manner of fruits, and yielding its fruit every month: and the leaves of the tree were for the healing of the nations." (Revelations 21 & 22)

FROM THE ENTIRE BIBLE WHICH WE SHALL here accept as a river of the Water of Life I have selected the most healing chapters and verses that are "as clear as crystal, proceeding out from the throne of God." Dip into these here and now, just as the spirit moves you. Immerse yourself completely in the entire stream whenever the deep yearning comes upon you. You cannot touch this stream at any point but you will find God. You cannot give yourself to its resistless flow at any place but you will find healing.

The flow of the stream is continuous, eternal, unending. Even when you are not dipping into it, the flow continues. It comes ever from the heart of God and enters into the heart of man, then it passes through the heart of man before it makes its return to the heart of God. Merely to touch it is to touch life and to immerse oneself in it is to experience what Paul meant when he said, "Pray without ceasing."

FIRST MEDITATION

"For Ye Are the Children of God"

1. What is man that Thou art mindful of him? . . . Thou hast made him a little lower than the angels, and crownest him with glory and honor. Thou makest him to have dominion . . . (Ps. 8:4-6 R.V.) . . . partakers of the divine nature. (2 Peter 1:4) Now we are the sons of God, (I John 3:2) in Christ, (Rom. 12:5) hid with Christ in God, (Col. 3:3) the power of God and the wisdom of God. (I Cor. 1:24)

2. The Lord possessed me in the beginning of His way . . . While as yet He had not made the earth . . . When He prepared the heavens, I was there . . . When He appointed the foundation of the earth: then I was by Him as one brought up with Him: and I was daily His delight, rejoicing always before Him. (Prov. 8:22, 26, 27, 29-31)

3. We are the children of God: And if children, then heirs; heirs of God, and joint-heirs with Christ. (Rom. 8:16, 17) In Him we live and move and have our being. (Acts 17:28) God created man in His own image. (Gen. 1:27) And God created man to be immortal and made him to be an image of His own eternity. (Wisdom of Solomon 2:23) Ye are gods, and the scriptures cannot be broken. (John 10:34) Ye are of God . . . greater is He that is in you, than he that is in the world. (I John 4:14) For ye are all the children of God. (Gal. 3:26)

4. I am the vine, ye are the branches: He that abideth in Me, and I in him, the same bringeth forth much fruit. (John 15:5) Ye have not chosen Me, but I have chosen you, and ordained you, that ye should go and bring forth fruit, and that your fruit should remain; that whatsoever ye shall ask of the Father in My name, He may give it you. (John 15:16)

SECOND MEDITATION

"I Am Fearfully and Wonderfully Made"

5. I will praise Thee; for I am fearfully and wonderfully made: marvelous are Thy works; and that my soul knoweth right well. My substance was not hid from Thee, when I was made in secret, and curiously wrought in the lowest parts of the earth. Thine eyes did see my substance, yet being unperfect; and in Thy book all my members were written, which in continuance were fashioned, when as yet there was none of them. How precious also are Thy thoughts unto me, O God! . . . if I should count them, they are more in number than the sand. (Ps. 139:14-18)

6. Behold, Thou desirest truth in the inward parts and in the hidden part Thou wilt make me to know wisdom. Purify me with hyssop, and I shall be clean: wash me, and I will be whiter than snow. Make me to hear joy and gladness; that my heart which is cast down may rejoice. Hide Thy face from my sins, and blot out all my iniquities. Create in me a clean heart, O God; and renew a right spirit within me. (Ps. 51:6-10)

7. Bless the Lord, O my soul: and all that is within me, bless His holy name. Bless the Lord, O my soul, and forget not all His benefits: Who forgiveth all thine iniquities; who

healeth all thy diseases; Who redeemeth thy life from destruction; who crowneth thee with lovingkindness and tender mercies; Who satisfieth thee with good things; so that thy youth is renewed like the eagle's. (Ps. 103:1-5)

THIRD MEDITATION

"Our Wrestling Is Not Against Flesh and Blood"

8. Be strong therefore in the Lord, and in the strength of His might. Put on the whole armour of God, that ye may be able to stand against the wiles of the adversary. For our wrestling is not against flesh and blood, but against the principalities, against the powers, against the world-rulers of this darkness, against the spiritual hosts of wickedness in high places. Wherefore take up the whole armour of God, that ye may be able to withstand in the evil day, and, having overcome all, to stand.

9. Stand therefore, having girded your loins with truth, and having put on the breastplate of righteousness, and having shod your feet with the equipment of the gospel of peace; over all taking up the shield of faith, wherewith ye shall be able to quench all the fiery darts of the evil one. And take the helmet of salvation and the sword of the Spirit, which is the word of God: with all prayer and supplication praying at all seasons in the Spirit, and watching thereunto in all perseverance. (Eph. 6:10-18)

10. For though we walk in the flesh, we do not war after the flesh: for the weapons of our warfare are not carnal, but mighty through God to the pulling down of strongholds; casting down imaginations, and every high thing that exalt-eth itself against the knowledge of God, and bringing into

captivity every thought to the obedience of Christ. (II Cor. 10:3-5)

11. Finally brethren, whatsoever things are true, whatsoever things are honorable, whatsoever things are just, whatsoever things are pure, whatsoever things are lovely, whatsoever things are of good report; think on these things. (Phil. 4:8)

12. May you be so rooted and grounded in Love, that you can comprehend with all God's people what is the meaning of the breadth, the length, the depth, the height, by knowing the love of Christ which passes all knowledge, that ye be filled with the entire fullness of God.

Now to Him that is able to do exceedingly, abundantly above all that we ask or think, according to the power that worketh in us, unto Him be the glory in the Church and in Jesus Christ unto all generations for ever and ever. Amen. (Eph. 3:14-21)

FOURTH MEDITATION

"Love Never Faileth"

13. Though I speak with the tongues of men and of angels, but have not love, I am become sounding brass, or a clanging cymbal. And though I have the gift of prophecy, and understand all mysteries and all knowledge; and though I have all faith, so that I could remove mountains, but have not love, I am nothing.

14. Love suffereth long, and is kind, love envieth not; love vaunteth not itself, is not puffed up, doth not behave itself unseemly, seeketh not its own, is not easily provoked, think-

eth no evil; rejoiceth not in unrighteousness, but rejoiceth with the truth; beareth all things, believeth all things, hopeth all things, endureth all things.

15. Love never faileth: but whether there be prophecies, they shall fail; whether there be tongues, they shall cease; whether there be knowledge, it shall be done away. For we know in part, and we prophesy in part: but when that which is perfect is come, that which is in part will be done away.

16. When I was a child, I spake as a child, I felt as a child, I thought as a child: now that I am become a man, I have put away childish things. For now we see in a mirror darkly; but then face to face; now I know in part; but then I shall know even as also I have been known. And now abideth faith, hope, love, these three; and the greatest of these is love. (I Cor. 13)

FIFTH MEDITATION

"Be Not Anxious for Your Life"

17. Lay not up for yourselves treasures upon the earth, where moth and rust doth consume, and where thieves break through and steal: but lay up for yourselves treasures in heaven, where neither moth nor rust doth consume, and where thieves do not break through and steal: for where thy treasure is, there will thy heart be also.

18. Therefore I say unto you, Be not anxious for your life, What ye shall eat, or what ye shall drink; nor yet for your body, what ye shall put on. Is not life more than meat, and the body than raiment? Behold the fowls of the air: for they sow not, neither do they reap, nor gather in barns; yet their heavenly Father feedeth them. Are not ye of much

more value than they? And which of you by being anxious
can add one cubit unto his stature? And why are ye anxious
concerning raiment? Consider the lilies of the field, how
they grow; they toil not, neither do they spin: and yet I
say unto you, Even Solomon in all his glory was not arrayed
like one of these. Wherefore, if God so clothe the grass of
the field which today is, and tomorrow is cast into the oven,
shall he not much more clothe you, O ye of little faith?

19. Be not therefore anxious, saying, What shall we eat?
or, what shall we drink, or Wherewithal shall we be clothed?
For all these things do the nations of the world seek after:
for your heavenly Father knoweth that ye have need of all
these things. But seek ye first the kingdom of God, and his
righteousness; and all these things shall be added unto you.
(Matt. 6:19-21; 25-33)

Sixth Meditation

"He That Dwelleth in the Secret Place of the Most High"

20. He that dwelleth in the secret place of the Most High
Shall abide under the shadow of the Almighty,
I will say of the Lord, He is my refuge and my fortress;
My God, in whom I trust.
Surely He shall deliver thee from the snare of the fowler,
And from the noisome pestilence.
He shall cover thee with his pinions,
And under His wings shalt thou take refuge:
His truth shall be thy shield and buckler.

21. Thou shalt not be afraid for the terror by night;
Nor for the arrow that flieth by day;

For the pestilence that walketh in darkness,
Nor for the destruction that wasteth at noonday.
Though a thousand fall at thy side,
And ten thousand at thy right hand;
It shall not come nigh thee.

22. Because thou hast made the Lord,
Even the Most High, thy habitation;
There shall no evil befall thee,
Neither shall any plague come nigh thy dwelling.
For He shall give his angels charge over thee,
To keep thee in all thy ways.
Upon their hands they shall bear thee,
Lest thou dash thy foot against a stone.
Thou shalt tread upon the lion and adder:
The young lion and the dragon shalt thou trample under
    foot.

23. Even because he hath set his love upon Me, saith the
    Lord, therefore will I deliver him:
I will set him on high, because he hath known My name.
He shall call upon Me, and I will answer him;
I will be with him in trouble:
I will deliver him, and honour him.
With long life will I satisfy him
And shew him My salvation.

(Ps. 91)

SEVENTH MEDITATION

"Underneath Are the Everlasting Arms"

24. Be not afraid of sudden fear. (Prov. 3:25) For God
hath not given us the spirit of fear but of power and of love,

and of a sound mind. (II Tim. 1:7) For I the Lord thy God will hold thy right hand, saying unto thee, Fear not, I will help thee. (Isa. 41:13) When thou liest down, thou shalt not be afraid: and thy sleep shall be sweet. (Prov. 3:24) The eternal God is thy dwelling place, and underneath are the everlasting arms. (Deut. 33:27, E.R.V.)

25. Come unto me all ye that labor and are heavy laden, and I will give you rest. Take My yoke upon you, and learn of Me; for I am meek and lowly in heart; and ye shall find rest unto your souls. For My yoke is easy and my burden light. (Matt. 11:28-30) I am the Lord that healeth thee. (Ex. 15:26) Before they call, I will answer. (Isa. 65:24) Unto you that fear My name shall the Sun of righteousness arise with healing in its wings. (Mal. 4:2) Call unto me, and I will answer thee, and show thee great and mighty things which thou knowest not. (Jer. 33:3)

26. The Lord is good, a stronghold in the day of trouble; and He knoweth them that trust in Him. (Nah. 1:7) As for God, His way is perfect; the word of the Lord is tried; He is a shield unto all them that take refuge in Him. (II Sam. 22:31, E.R.V.)

27. I will restore health unto thee, and I will heal thee of thy wounds, saith the Lord. (Jer. 30:17) Not by might, not by power, but by My Spirit, said the Lord of hosts. (Zech. 4:6) Let Him take hold of My strength. (Isa. 27:5) I have heard thy prayer, I have seen thy tears: behold, I will heal thee. (II Kings 20:5) Behold, I will bring health and cure, and I will cure them; and will reveal unto them abundance of peace and truth. (Jer. 33:6)

28. My God shall supply all your need according to His riches in glory by Jesus Christ. (Phil. 4:19) For God is not the author of confusion, but of peace. (I Cor. 14:33) Acquaint now thyself with Him, and be at peace, thereby good shall come unto thee. (Job. 22:21) And the peace of God, which passeth all understanding, shall guard your hearts and your thoughts in Christ Jesus. (Phil. 4:7, E.R.V.)

29. My soul shall be satisfied as with marrow and fatness; and my mouth shall praise Thee with joyful lips; when I remember Thee upon my bed, and meditate on Thee in the night watches. For Thou hast been my help, and in the shadow of Thy wings will I rejoice. (Ps. 63)

EIGHTH MEDITATION

"All Things Work Together for Good to Them That Love God"

30. Come now and let us reason together, saith the Lord: though your sins be as scarlet, they shall be white as snow: though they be red like crimson, they shall be as wool. (Isa. 1:18) I have blotted out as a thick cloud, thy transgressions, and, as a cloud, thy sins. Return unto Me, for I have redeemed thee. (Isa. 44:22) And the spirit of the Lord will come upon thee, and thou . . . shalt be turned into another man. (I Sam. 10:6) For as the heavens are high above the earth, so great is His mercy toward them that fear Him. As far as the east is from the west, so far hath He removed our transgressions from us. (Ps. 103:11, 12)

31. Ye shall seek Me, and find Me, when ye search for Me with all your heart. (Jer. 29:13) Every good gift and every perfect boon is from above, coming down from the

Father of lights, with Whom can be no variation, neither shadow that is cast by turning. (Jas. 1:17) The Lord is nigh unto all them that call upon Him, to all that call upon Him in truth. He will fulfill the desire of them that fear Him, He also will hear their cry and will save them. The Lord preserveth all them that love Him. (Ps. 145:18-20) Delight thyself also in the Lord; and He shall give thee the desires of thine heart. Commit thy ways unto the Lord; trust also in Him; and He will bring it to pass. (Ps. 37:4, 5) All things work together for good to them that love God. (Rom. 8:28)

32. Glorify God in your body. (I Cor. 6:20) Wherefore make straight the hands that hang down, and the palsied knees; and make straight paths for your feet, that that which is lame be not put out of joint, but rather be healed. (Heb. 12:12, 13, E.R.V.) The Eternal God is thy refuge. (Deut. 33:27) It is He that giveth thee power. (Deut. 8:18) Who healeth all thy diseases: Who satisfieth thy mouth with good things: so that thy youth is renewed like the eagle. (Ps. 103: 3, 5) I will take sickness away from the midst of thee. (Ex. 23:25-6) As thy days, so shall thy strength be. (Deut. 33:25)

33. Be still, and know that I am God. (Ps. 46:10) Thou wilt keep him in perfect peace whose mind is stayed on Thee because he trusteth in Thee. (Isa. 26:3) Peace I leave with you, My peace I give unto you: not as the world giveth, give I unto you. Let not your heart be troubled, neither let it be afraid. (John 14:27) For thus saith the Lord God, the Holy one of Israel; in returning and rest shall ye be saved; in quietness and in confidence shall be your strength. (Isa. 30:15) My presence shall go with thee, and I will give thee rest. (Ex. 33:14)

34. Oh that men would praise the Lord for his loving-kindness, and for His wonderful works to the children of men! For He satisfieth the longing soul, And the hungry soul He filleth with good. (Ps. 107)

NINTH MEDITATION

"With God All Things Are Possible"

35. And when ye stand praying, forgive, if ye have aught against any: that your Father also which is in heaven may forgive you your trespasses. (Mark 11:25) Let all bitterness, and wrath, and anger, and clamor, and evil speaking be put away from you, with all malice. (Eph. 4:31) Release, and ye shall be released. (Luke 6:37, E.R.V.)

36. And God saw everything that He had made, and, behold, it was very good. (Gen. 1:31) Whatsoever God doeth, it shall be forever; Nothing can be put to it, nor anything taken from it. (Eccl. 3:14) In the Lord Jehovah is everlasting strength. (Isa. 26:4) The same yesterday, and today, and forever. (Heb. 13:8) Commit thy works unto the Lord, and thy purposes shall be established. (Prov. 16:3, E.R.V.) With God all things are possible. (Matt. 19:26) If ye abide in Me, and My words abide in you, Ye shall ask what ye will, and it shall be done unto you. (John 15:7)

37. Your joy no man taketh from you. (John 16:22) The joy of the Lord is your strength. (Neh. 8:10) Therefore did my heart rejoice, and my tongue was glad; moreover also my flesh shall rest in hope. (Acts 2:26) In the shadow of Thy wings will I rejoice. (Ps. 63:7) Thou wilt show me the path of life: in Thy presence is the fulness of joy: at Thy right hand there are pleasures for evermore. (Ps. 16:11)

38. Then shall thy light break forth as the morning, and thy healing shall spring forth speedily; and thy righteousness shall go before thee; the glory of the Lord shall be thy guard. (Isa. 58:8) Thy faith hath saved thee; go in peace. (Luke 7:50) I will restore health unto thee. (Jer. 30:17) Behold, thou art made whole. (John 5:14)

39. It is a good thing to give thanks unto the Lord, and to sing praises unto Thy name, O Most High; To shew forth Thy lovingkindness in the morning, and Thy faithfulness every night. For Thou, Lord, hast made me glad through Thy work: I will triumph in the work of Thy hands. (Ps. 92)

IX. BATHS OF HEALING

<><><><><><><><><><><><><><><><><><><><><><><><><><><><><><><><>

The Parable of the Little Child in
the Back Yard Swing

Once upon a time there was a great philosopher who had devoted many years to finding the secret of life. One day he turned in at a gate to visit a sick neighbor who craved the strength his presence would bring. When he saw the neighbor's child amusing himself in the back yard swing, he seated himself on a bench and looked at the child.

"My sick friend has been seeking all his life to find the secret of keeping in tune with the Heavens," he thought to himself, "and here in his own back yard he could find the answer. This child has already learned the secret as he 'works up' in the swing. To rise high depends upon his ability to give himself unresistingly to the upward and downward movement of the swing. Nothing could make the 'old cat die' so quickly as to put oneself in opposition to this upward and downward momentum. In the same way nothing will make one's joy in living and one's hold on life 'die' so quickly as to put oneself into opposition to the great inner rhythm of the heavens.

"And what is the rhythm of the heavens? It is the rhythm that regulates and controls all of life's processes from the

greatest to the least: the alternation of day with night, the coming and going of the seasons, the waxing and waning of the moon, the ebb and flow of the tide, the systole and diastole of the heart, the inspiration and expiration of the breath. And what is the principle behind this rhythm? It is very simple, washing out the discarded, the old, the bad; and washing in the fresh, the new, the good. Do this and thou shalt live."

The wise man lifted up his eyes in gratitude towards the heavens. As he did so he saw in the west the sun setting in a blaze of gold; in the east a moon exposing its silver crescent to the eyes of men. "The two lights, the greater and the lesser," he thought to himself, "represent those two poles of the rhythm of the heavens. The moon represents the negative, protective, cleansing pole of this irresistible healing harmony. The sun represents the positive pole of the cosmic harmony—the pole of the creative, strengthening, healing forces of life. Sweep out the evil; sweep in the good. Put oneself in tune with the eternal forces and we have learned the secret of the ages."

So the wise man arose and went in to see his sick friend, knowing that the same law prevails, whether it be in the back yard swing of the little child, or in the cosmic movement of the planetary system. And that law is that with every breath we cast out that which would destroy life and with every breath we drink in that which would fulfill life.

IF YOU ARE SICK AND WISH TO BE WELL, ALL you need to do is to breathe out the bad and breathe in the good. In other words, step into harmony with the back yard swing, into harmony with the healing forces in the Kingdom of Heaven itself.

In this chapter I present one method by which this may be done. In an earlier chapter (page 88) I defined the three methods of prayer in Jesus' statement, "ask . . . seek . . . knock," as the prayer of petition, the prayer of meditation, and the prayer of denial and affirmation. Because the last method is usually the most effective for beginners, I have chosen to use it here.

When Dante entered the Earthly Paradise he had to be completely immersed in two rivers, Lethe and Eunoe. In the first he was washed of all remembrance of the bad; in the other he was filled with the realization of all that was good. There is something fundamental and absolute about this rhythm which I cannot and will not try to explain, that is helpful to the one who is in trouble.

The following exercises, based upon this fundamental rhythm of Lethe and Eunoe are offered as aids to those who are in great need of help and do not know where to begin. The numbers refer back to passages from the Scriptures in the last chapter.

For one who is ill and striving to pack his mind and heart with beautiful, constructive thoughts, I cannot recommend any finer exercise than to memorize passages that are specially helpful and repeat them many, many times a day. It is often the experience of one who has traveled the same path many times that some day he awakens to find that at last he can travel it with "hind's feet." When that is accomplished, then the Lord will deliver him from his afflictions and will "set him upon his high places."

The list of troubles has been arranged alphabetically. I shall illustrate the use that may be made of the exercises by commenting somewhat in detail upon the first one, which is a set of "exercises" to safeguard one against

Accidents: The best protection against accidents is to clear the atmosphere within and without of all angers, fears and thoughts of violence. There always are some aspects of danger when young people start on an auto journey while the parents are engaged in a violent quarrel. There is very little danger of an airplane accident when all those traveling are in a happy, loving mood, and all their friends and well-wishers back home are praying for them with happy, harmonious thoughts. A French Senator wrote me shortly after Lindbergh's epoch-making flight, "There are many in Paris who believe that it was not the plane that brought Lindbergh, it was Lindbergh who brought the plane."

"Exercise" for protection against accidents:

Immersion in River Lethe (Erasing the Bad): Realize that there is no discord, no misunderstanding in heaven.

Immersion in Eunoe (Realization of the Good): Realize that all is harmony, happiness and peace. As God controls the stars in their courses, so He can direct our paths so that there will be no collision or discord of any kind.

Read sections in the preceding chapter: 8, 9, 18, 19, 22, 28, 31, 39.

Anemia and trouble in circulation of blood: There is nothing to block the perfect circulation of joy which always is flowing with perfect ease and perfect power, for joy is always projected through the channels of consciousness by the power of love and love is omnipotent, for love is God. Read: 25, 2, 5, 37, 38, 39.

Appendicitis (or gall-bladder troubles): There is no frustration, no repressed resentments in heaven, all is forgiveness, love, holiness and purity. There is no stagnation. All of God's ideas flow with perfect regularity and ease, for all ideas in heaven are propelled by love and love is infinite for love is God. Read: 5, 6, 35, 10, 11, 12.

Arthritis: There is nothing bound or rigid in heaven, no self will, all is God's will, no stubbornness, resentment or unforgiveness. One's heart and will and mind are free and flowing and fluid, receptive to the least, little loving wish of God. Read: 35, 20, 22, 32, 7, 26, 18.

Asthma: There is no self-pity in heaven; no undue leaning on friends, for the Infinite Love encompasses and nourishes all and God always takes care of His own. God breathes through His children with unfailing regularity and ease, bringing peace and happiness to all. Read: 24, 20, 21, 22, 18, 8, 9, 27, 28.

Blindness: There is no blindness in heaven for man has infinite capacity to see and to understand God's ideas. Man is ever beholding the glory of God and the beauty of His handiwork. "The hearing ear and the seeing eye, the Lord hath made even both of them." (Prov. 20:12) Read: 17, 18, 19, 20, 22, 27, 38.

Cancer: There is no bitterness in heaven, all is forgiveness, harmony, and peace. No sense of injustice, for what is taken from one in injustice is returned sixtyfold by another channel if one keeps the channels clear and forgiving. Man is the reflection of love, reflecting only kindness, and gentleness and compassion. Read: 3, 6, 12, 23, 26.

Children's diseases: No evil can touch children in the Kingdom, "for their angels (thoughts) are always beholding the Father." There is no discord or fear in the home of children for all is harmony, peace, and love, and love is the power that holds all things in perfectly adjusted and harmonious relationship. Read: 21, 22, 3, 18.

Common cold: There is no congestion in heaven, no undue thought of self. One's thoughts are always God's thoughts, and His ways our ways. Read: 5, 6, 3, 11, 27, 39.

Constipation: There is no inhibition or withholding of any kind in heaven, all ideas pass with unfailing regularity and ease. The perfect ideas of God are properly grouped and circulate eternally in perfect sequence and order. Read: 17, 19, 5, 6.

Deafness: There is no deafness in heaven, for man has infinite capacity to hear and to understand God's ideas. Man is God's consciousness, always listening to God and not one of God's ideas is ever lost. "The hearing ear and the seeing eye, the Lord hath made even both of them." (Prov. 20:12) Read: 17, 18, 19, 20, 22, 28, 31.

Diarrhoea: There is no disgust or discord in heaven, no expulsion in heaven, no nausea in heaven, for all is governed by God, the principle of all law and order. God's ideas never pass prematurely but unfold with perfect sequence and perfect regularity. Read: 5, 6, 36.

Diabetes: There is no lack of the sweetness and completeness of life, for all God's Universe is instantly available and continuously unfolding to man's experience in perfect sequence and perfect rhythm just as rapidly as His capacity to assimilate and appropriate it for unselfish use will permit. Read: 1, 2, 3, 4, 17, 19.

Epilepsy: There is no evil power at work in heaven, the only power is God and His control over all things is unceasing and uninterrupted. "When He giveth quietness, who then can make trouble?" (Job 34:29) Read: 1, 8, 9, 18, 19, 24, 33.

Growths (tumors, goitres, etc.): There are no abnormal growths in heaven; one always has his own which no one can take from him. There is no envy or jealousy which draws to one that which does not belong to him. Read: 1, 2, 3, 4, 31.

Heart trouble: There is no lack or limitation of love in heaven. It continually flows in perfect rhythm and perfect strength, in perfect sequence and perfect order, continually bringing harmony, unity, and happiness to all. Read: 13, 19, 15, 26.

Indigestion: There is no difficulty in assimilating ideas in heaven, no fear, no confusion, all is clear and man loves to receive the ideas of God which he assimilates, digests, and understands and groups together into perfect combinations which radiate out in the All-Mind giving infinite beings joy and happiness. There is no sense of inadequacy for when man works God works. God's work is always done by means of love made manifest in man. Read: 18, 19, 33, 5, 6, 10, 11.

Influenza: There is no hate or fear in heaven, no fatigue; one is always resting in the healing arms of the Father. The congested hate and fear thoughts of mankind cannot penetrate one who abides in the Secret Place of the Most High, for nothing passes to man except God's ideas which always are spiritual, perfect, holy, pure and divine. Read: 5, 6, 3, 9, 28, 33.

Kidney troubles: There is no congestion of self, no impurity in heaven. All is pure Spirit filling man with all purity and holiness. Man is made in the image and likeness of God, pure and eternal. Read: 5, 6, 10, 11, 35, 12, 32, 3.

Laryngitis: Nothing man does is ever futile for God is always doing work by means of man and does everything in love, permanently, harmoniously and completely. Read: 12, 13, 14, 15, 16.

Liver troubles: There is no passing of unkind judgments in heaven for everyone in heaven is a perfect being in a perfect universe governed by a perfect God. Read: 18, 19, 33, 5, 6, 32.

Menopause: There is no change of life in heaven, for God is life "from ever-lasting to ever-lasting" (Ps. 90:2) "the same yesterday, today and forever." (Heb. 13:8) There is no power in one organ to upset the functions of other organs. God is the only power and His control is the control of love, and love is the power that brings all things into perfectly adjusted and harmonious relationship. Read: 28, 5, 20, 21, 22, 23.

Mental troubles: Man never can be out of his mind in heaven, for man always abides in the mind of God, and God is always sane, always well, always perfect. Man has no mind of his own, his mind is God's Mind, unchanging and eternal. There are no illusions, no part truths, no "demons," God is the whole truth and the whole truth shall make you whole and free. Read: 31, 20, 21, 22, 23, 25, 27, 28, 33, 36.

Nerves: There are no tense nerves in heaven, man's nerves are the spiritual and divine channels in consciousness whereby God's ideas come to man, giving him continuous joy and happiness. Read: 24, 20, 21, 22, 28, 25, 33.

Pneumonia: There is no fear or discouragement in heaven, no thoughts of self of any kind. Man's breathing is the spontaneous activity of the love of God and the life of the Holy Spirit, always perfect and joyous, for man is the Son of God and God is always breathing through love made manifest in man. Read: 6, 20, 21, 22, 23, 33.

Rheumatism: There is no criticism or cynicism in heaven, for man is perfect and man knows that man is perfect, man is divine and man knows that man is divine. One is always willing to move from one idea to another freely and easily with no stubbornness or rebellion for God is the source of all the ideas that come to man. Read: 35, 32, 5, 13, 16, 12, 36.

Sinus trouble: There is no inflammation or blockage in heaven, no self will, all is God's will. We abide in God and He in us. We are one with all that is good. God's healing love fills us and abides in us bringing peace, and love and comfort. Man always achieves what God wishes him to achieve, easily and effortlessly. Read: 5, 6, 9, 11, 27, 29, 38.

Skin irritations: The loving, protective covering of God preserves and maintains man's individuality. There can be no irritation or disturbance for man is always protected by the soothing, healing unfoldment of God's infinite love, for love guides, controls and governs every idea in the Universe giving joy and happiness. Read: 20, 21, 22, 24, 25, 26, 27, 28, 29, 33, 19.

Stone in kidney; stone in liver and gall bladder: There is no frustration, no hoarding of unhappy ideas in heaven, man is governed by God, always helping his fellow man, passing on God's ideas of abundance and plenty giving his fellow man joy and happiness. Read: 17, 19, 5, 6, 16.

Tonsilitis and quinsy: There are no repressed resentments or fears in heaven. All that we should achieve we shall achieve, if we repose all in God's hands. Read: 5, 6, 35, 10, 11, 12.

Tuberculosis: There are no unappeased yearnings for affections in heaven, no eating out of one's heart for self-expression. All fulfillment is God's fulfillment. God breathes through His children with unfailing regularity and ease, bringing peace, holiness and wholeness. Breathing is the spontaneous activity of life and love, perfect and joyous. Read: 5, 6, 7, 20, 21, 22, 23, 27.

Typhoid fever: There is no tension in heaven. Man is God's channel in consciousness eternally relaxed to heaven's perfect ideas which flow in perfect sequence and perfect order. No poison of fear or of self can enter God's perfect channels, for these channels are governed by love and love casteth out all fear, for love is omnipotent, for love is God. Read: 6, 18, 19, 20, 21, 22, 30.

ADDICTIONS

To Criticism: One cannot see imperfections in heaven for each one is a child of God, governed by Divine Love and all ideas are circulated and directed by the impulse of love. Read: 13, 14, 15, 16, 35, 36, 39.

To Depression: Man never fails for man is the knowledge of God and God always does His will through love made manifest in man. All is perfect, harmonious, and beautiful, and the imperfections in life are merely the fogs created by one's own wrong thinking. Read: 25, 21, 22, 1, 2, 3, 4.

To Drinking: Man is a son of God and cannot possibly be a slave to shadows and counterfeit of reality. God is the only power the only control and the only Master, and is always sending inspiration to His children just as they need it. Read: 31, 6, 8, 9, 22, 26, 30.

To Lying: There is no untruth in heaven, for God is truth. "Ye shall know the truth and the truth shall make you free." (John 8:32) God's world is so perfect and His plan for each so wonderful that merely to see this plan in all its beauty and perfection transcends anything man's mind could imagine or tongue express. Read: 30, 31, 6, 8, 9, 22.

To Sex: Man is not in bondage to any physical desire for

man is the child of God, eternally united in spirit with Him.
There are no impure thoughts, for man is spiritual, perfect,
holy, and divine, and can only see others as holy, pure and
divine. Read: 30, 10, 6, 11, 5, 22, 26.

To Stealing: Man can never take things from his fellow
men for all God's ideas are in the right place and to take
that which is not one's own is to rob oneself. One is never
in need of anything for there are infinite ideas available and
man grows by giving and not by taking. Read: 30, 31, 6, 8,
9, 22.

To Worry: Man need never worry for man is a child of
God, impervious as in a citadel, for no evil can touch him
when he rests in God. Read: 24, 18, 19, 21, 22, 28, 33.

IMPORTANT

1. Remember that the assertions in this chapter are merely
to liberate your consciousness from the prison-like feeling
that you have to be sick.

VERY IMPORTANT

2. Remember that the numbers which refer to the Scrip-
tural passages in Chapter VIII are true words of healing.
Memorize some of these so that you can say them day or
night. Browse through the entire chapter from time to time
marking other passages which especially raise your consciousness, and refer to them often.

Re-read Chapters VI and VII, particularly the former,
marking any passages that will help you to rise to the place
where you can "relinquish" your illness away, or, better
still, "*know*" it away.

STILL MORE IMPORTANT

3. Remember to accept your illness as a "telephone message" that is sent to protect you from other evils worse than the illness itself. Pray with more sincerity and earnestness for liberation from these evils that may threaten your heart and soul than for liberation from the evils that threaten the body.

MOST IMPORTANT OF ALL

4. Remember that life-time habits of wrong thinking and their consequent body reactions cannot always be eradicated in one day. If you are really in earnest about getting well and staying well, definitely plan a three months' regime of mental and spiritual discipline.

In *I Will Lift Up Mine Eyes* I have arranged "Stair-ways" for lifting your consciousness to the place where your dreams may come true. I also suggest the practice of carrying for frequent reference in idle moments a booklet of pocket-size, such as *The Lord's Prayer*, or *Songs of the Souls of Men*, or Drummond's *Greatest Thing in the World*, or Brother Lawrence's *The Practice of the Presence of God.**

APPENDIX:
THE WITNESS OF ORIENTAL MYSTICISM

The Parable of Two Groups Digging
One Tunnel

*Once upon a time two groups of workers started at oppo-
site sides of a mountain, miles apart, each paying no heed
to what the other group was doing, but each following
faithfully a blueprint of its own. One day both groups met
in the very center of the mountain, and lo, their tunnels,
without missing one inch, fitted together perfectly, as if one
group had bored the single passage.*

*Not far away two other groups are now boring from
opposite directions to build another tunnel. The mountain
they are trying to master is not a mountain of earth and
stone, but a mountain of disease and death. One group tun-
neling from one direction, is dealing with the unseen elements of the body, eliminating death-dealing microbes and
germs; the other penetrating from the other direction is
dealing with the invisible elements of the soul, obliterating
the soul-killing emotions, the angers and fears, the envies
and lusts of the world. This wall is no more impenetrable
than the wall of earth and stone that separated the Cascade
tunnelers. The time may soon come when these two groups
may meet on common ground.*

And what will hasten that time?

It will be by the doctors giving respect and considera-
tion for the work of the ministers and the ministers giving
respect and consideration for the work of the doctors, yet
each doing his own work as conscientiously and as faithfully
as he knows how.

Then, like the two bands of workers who found that their
separate tunnels ultimately formed one great Cascade
Tunnel, it will be proved, through honest, faithful work,
with mutual respect and trust in each other, each living up
to the best light which it is given, that those who serve in
the field of medicine and those who serve in the field of
religion have been working upon the same pattern, follow-
ing the same blueprint for creating a world where men may
become both holy and whole.

THE ORIENTAL MIND THROUGHOUT THE AGES
has not been as interested in the outer body as it has been in
the inner soul. While Western science explored man's physical organs, the Eastern philosophy explored man's psychic
centers.

Western science studied the secret and mysteries of man's
skin, then of his arteries, then of his nervous system, then
of his vital organs. But when Western science reached man's
glands, it stopped, baffled. The full mystery attending these
unique organs never has been completely explained. They
represent a frontier opening up an entirely unexplored
universe.

Oriental philosophers studied man's soul, but when it
came to the study of the body, as far as it went was to discover seven "centers" through which the spirit and soul
poured its power into the body.

Just recently there has come a realization that the seven
glands of Western science and the seven centers of Eastern
occultism may have a relationship which, when properly
understood, might explain the relationship between the soul
and the body, the seen and the unseen. They stand like seven
sentinels facing each other across the no man's land that
unites soul and body.

Let us consider for a moment the remarkable functions of
these glands. Secreted in the ductless glands are to be found
the most amazing, miracle-working elements the world has
ever known. For centuries alchemists have tried to learn the
secret of converting other elements into gold. But all the
miracles of all the alchemists together pale into insignificance
before the marvelous miracles that God is working every day
through the means of the glands of the human body.

Take for example the secretions within the digestive glands. A delicious sliver of potato touches a man's lips, and instantly these miracle-producing glands send into circulation a magic substance which almost instantly transforms the food into a fluid substance which in turn is soon transformed into tissue of the body. A forkful of savory Boston baked beans follows the potato, and this time the action of the unseen glands converts the new material into muscle and gristle. Does not the simple little act of turning iron into gold pale into insignificance before such marvelous miracles as this?

Jesus represents in the Christian Church the mediator and emissary between God and man—the one person above all others who combined perfectly the elements of perfect man and perfect God. He represents in Christian theological thinking, the bridge between the unseen and the seen, the spiritual and the physical for most of us.

In the ancient Greek world the god Mercury took over that office for the devout of that day. He was called the messenger of the gods—the speedy comer, who brought the unseen message from Olympus down to man. Since that time science has named a substance after him, a substance which combines two elements—fluid and mineral—symbolic of the two fields, the earthly and the heavenly. As we use mercury in the thermometer and barometer to give us messages of what is going on in the unseen elements of air, to make them articulate and vocal to our physical understanding, so the substance within the glands of the human body acts as a thermometer and barometer of conditions that are transpiring in our mental and emotional natures. If properly understood, nothing can give us any better guidance, of the state of the human body in all its relations and activities in life.

But why listen to me on this subject, why not listen to a famous doctor of medicine who can speak with authority of the laboratory behind him. Writes Dr. Louis Berman in *The Glands Regulating Personality.*

The most precious bit of knowledge we possess today about Man is that he is the creature of his glands of internal secretion. That is, Man as a distinctive organism is the product, the by-product, of a number of cell factories which control the parts of his make-up, much as the different divisions of an automobile concern produce the different parts of a car. These chemical factories consist of cells which manufacture special substances, which act upon the other cells of the body, and so start and determine the countless processes we call Life. Life, body and soul emerge from the activities of the magic ooze of their silent chemistry precisely as a tree of tin crystals arises from the chemical reactions started in a solution of tin salts by an electric current.

Man is regulated by his Glands of Internal Secretions. At the beginning of the third decade of the twentieth century, after he had struggled, for we know at least fifty thousand years, to define and know himself, that summary may be accepted as the truth about himself. It is a far-reaching induction, but a valid induction, supported by a multitude of detailed facts.

Let us pause in wonder for just a moment before the marvelous function of the secretions of the gonads. These glands are as different in male and female as the positive and negative elements of the electric magnet are different. When the secretions of one pole mingle with those of the other we witness a miracle that as far transcends the miracle we have just cited, of converting potatoes and beans into flesh and blood, as the light of the sun transcends the light of the moon. Out of the nowhere, yes, out of the heavenly sphere itself, they produce an actual living being!

Go further and witness the miracles produced by the other glands: how, for instance, the secretions of the thyroid gland can convert an idiot into a man of genius, how the secretions released from the adrenal glands can convert a coward into a hero, and so on and on. In fact, a few moments of careful study of the glands reveals that we have stepped into a positive world of fairyland, into a new world, where miracles are as common as breathing and as simple as the air we breathe.

In order to conceive how such miracles can come to pass we shall have to conceive of the glands as connecting links with some source of power outside and far away from the little human body itself. In order to conceive of this more clearly, let us think for a moment of our body as a house, a dwelling not made with hands.

In my childhood days we could have built a wall around our home and had everything we needed. To light it up we would fill the lamps with kerosene. To warm it we would put wood in the stove and fireplace, or coal in the furnace. Water for washing dishes we would throw out the door. There was no telephone, no radio. When we wanted music some one would play the piano.

Today all things are different. When we want a light we push the button, and wires connected with the power plant miles way, light our house for us; when we want music we turn on the radio and an opera star in faraway New York City fills the room with his song. When we want heat, it is derived from fuel oil poured from a duct from outside the house. When we want to talk with a neighbor, he does not come to us; we ring him on the telephone. When we throw water out we merely throw it down the sink, and it flows into a great sewer system serving the entire city.

There are seven doorways, ductless glands—if you care to call them such—which connect our house with powers far beyond ourselves. The power of the great opera star, the miracle of his years of training is given to us by the turning of a button; the majestic power of the entire Mississippi, fed by mountain springs, by rain from the skies, is ours by the mere act of turning a switch to flood our rooms with light. And so on ad infinitum.

Long before the radio, the telephone or the electric light were invented, the Hindus conceived of the seven Soul Centers which not only correspond remarkably to these instruments in the home on one hand, but also to the ductless glands on the other.

Here is a list in three columns, of what we might term *Service Centers* in the house, *Soul Centers* in the cosmic self, *Gland Centers* in the physical self:

SERVICE CENTERS	GLAND CENTERS	BRINGS IDEAS (Through centers and glands)	SOUL CENTERS
1. RADIO Brings ideas from far away	PINEAL (Unknown)	Brings *Intuitive ideas* Capacity for *Inspiration*	HEAD
2. TELEPHONE Brings communication from far away	PITUITARY (Unknown)	Brings *logical ideas* Capacity to *think*	EYEBROWS
3. ELECTRIC LIGHT Brings light from far away	THYROID (Thyroxin)	Brings *perceptual ideas* Capacity to *observe*	THROAT

SERVICE CENTERS	GLAND CENTERS	BRINGS IDEAS (Through centers and glands)	SOUL CENTERS
4. OIL Brings heat from far away	THYMUS (Unknown)	Brings *ENERGY* Capacity *to do*	HEART
5. GAS Brings cooking power from far away	PANCREAS (Insulin)	Brings *sensation* Capacity to *assimilate*	SOLAR PLEXUS
6. WATER Brings drink from far away	ADRENALS (Adrenalin)	Brings *COURAGE* Capacity to *Struggle*	BASE OF SPINE
7. TELEVISION Brings living persons from far away	GONADS	Brings *creative new life*	SACRAL CENTER

Mrs. Alice Bailey, one of our clearest modern minds, has in her great book, *The Soul and Its Mechanism*, made a very thorough and painstaking analysis and comparison of the glands of the occidental science, with the soul centers of oriental philosophy:

When we compare the Eastern Doctrine of the seven centers with the Western Doctrine of glands [she writes], we find *first of all* a striking fact with regard to locality. The seven centers of force are to be found in the same region where the glands are located, and each center of force might well be (and according to the Indian teaching is) the source of power and of life for the corresponding gland.

A *second fact*, even more striking than the first, is that the *force centers which are awake conform to the glands whose functions are known* and of which most of the secretions, or hormones, have been discovered. The centres that are asleep, or awakening in advanced members of the race, conform to the glands whose functions are relatively unknown and whose secretions in the main have not been isolated. It will be noted, for example, that Dr. Berman states that the secretions of the pineal gland, one of the two in the pituitary body, and the thymus gland, are listed as unknown, as is the secretion of the cortex adrenal gland. These conform to the sleeping or awakening heart centre, throat centre, centre in the head, and at the base of the spine.

Is this an interesting coincidence? Or are we faced with the fact that in each case these glands with the undiscovered hormones, are allied to a centre which is asleep, not yet awakened in average humanity?

I believe it will eventually be established that the glands have been brought into being through the energy of the centres, for those centres which, in average humanity, are awake and functioning seem to be related to glands, whose peculiar secretion has been isolated, and its action in relation to the blood stream known, whilst those centres which are as yet asleep and undeveloped seem to be allied to glands whose secretion is only partially known or totally unknown. It is in any case worthy of consideration.

The Occidental psychologists are consequently right when they state that a man is what his glands make him, and that we are no better than our peculiar endocrine system. But the reason for this may lie in the correctness of the Oriental theory as to the force centres. The condition of the glands and their super-activity or sub-normality, and their right or wrong functioning may be determined by the state of those centres. *The glands are only outer symbols, the visible, material aspect of a far greater and more intricate system.* They are determined by the character of the soul life which plays through them, and the soul which controls and dominates all.

The state of the centres, then, is dependent upon the type and quality of soul force vibrating through them.

If we refer back to the excerpt from Dr. Louis Berman's famous book, *The Glands Regulating Personality*, on page 154 we find that the conclusion is drawn that man is the "creature of his glands of internal secretion," that "man as a distinctive organism is the product, the by-product, if we will, of a number of cell factories which control the parts of his makeup, much as the different parts of an automobile concern produce the different parts of a car."

I want to take a step beyond Dr. Berman at this point, and take my stand with Mrs. Bailey, in supporting the hypothesis that the glands are not the *source* of those products but rather the *instruments* for bringing these products to man. They are not the "factories" which produce but the "channels" which control the various parts of his make-up. Let me illustrate by a parable. The average man would say that the orange on the orange tree was produced by the "cell factories" within the tree, the leaves, buds, bark, roots, etc. A true scientist would say the leaves, trunk, roots and even the buds did not *produce* the orange, but that these elements were the instruments for gathering the moisture from the clouds, the sun rays from the sun and the chemical elements from the soil, which, combined together produce the orange.

Let us consider another parable. Suppose you had a radio within your house, catching a message from New York, a telephone receiving a message from Chicago, an electric light getting its light from Niagara, and so on. A native from South Africa who has never seen or even heard of a radio or telephone during his life, but who is familiar with mechanical devices of various kinds, comes to be your guest. He would naturally say at once that these various machines were little cell factories, "manufacturing" the sounds, and that the various speeches, messages, light, gas and heat were but the product, or by-product, of these cell factories situated in different parts of the house. Then you would smile at his ignorance and tell him that the symphony he hears in the parlor is this very minute being played by a hundred performers in a great music hall in New York, and that the voice he is hearing in the sitting room comes through a long-distance phone from Cleveland.

Now if we turn to the two sets of ductless glands, which represent the highest and lowest portions of the body, and examine their "products" we shall find, I am sure, that their wonder and mystery is far more easily and reasonably explained according to the channel hypothesis than by the hypothesis of the factory. For instance the "product" of the gonad glands is a baby, which appears in this world with a potential reasoning capacity, an intuitive capacity, a capacity to love, to lead, to create. Is it possible to say that a set of glands produced a creature "just a little lower than the angels," yes, even a "son of God"? Is it not absurd to say that a Lincoln, a Shakespeare, a Dante were the products of anything less than infinite powers that transcend space and time?

Why cannot we conceive that it is possible that the pineal gland is a radio receiving set for the bringing of such masterpieces of art as Hamlet, Othello or King Lear out of the infinite Mind of God? Or would we prefer to say that that mass of convolutions of the human brain, that organ which looks so much like a piece of cheese, can secrete ideas, much like the liver secretes bile? Can we say that this was the way such masterpieces as Homer's *Odyssey*, Dante's *Divine Comedy*, Milton's *Paradise Lost* were produced? If you examine the convolutions of the human brain with the pineal gland as the focus, you will find that it looks very much like the convolutions and batteries of the radio in your parlor, with its antennae focusing the sound. In other words, Edison was more nearly right than some of us supposed, when he said that he felt that *his invention came through him.* Expounding on this further he said that he felt that ideas are like oil in the depths of the earth, which come up through the highest hills. If the highest is not there it would come through the next highest. He said that if he had not lived, he felt that the 1500 inventions under his name would have come to the world through some other inventors, sooner or later.

For thirty years I have been a teacher of creative writing and reading. Among other things, I have made a careful and exhaustive study of the sources from whence great writers derive their power. With scarcely a single exception among all the great writers of all time I find that they ascribe their genius to a power outside of themselves. Socrates began it when he was announced as "the wisest of the Greeks because he knew that he knew nothing." Upon testing this out Socrates discovered that all other writers and philosophers, all the little half-baked geniuses, thought that their own little personal brains secreted ideas as the liver secretes bile. He alone knew that his brain was a mere receiving set through which the gods spoke, and all that he said or did that was worth while came not from himself, but from the infinite forces in the universe. Moses was outstanding among the Jews, and saved them when no one else was competent to do it, because he also knew that he knew nothing, but was merely a bush in the wilderness catching fire from heaven. If he was selfless enough, and transparent as the bush he saw, which was not destroyed when it caught fire, he could transmute that fire to the hearts and minds of men. By the way, this is a beautiful symbolical description of that great modern miracle, the incandescent lamp bulb, which, being emptied of itself, can carry a light from the power house. The man who imagines that his own brain produces his poems and inventions, produces a light comparable to the flickering light of a candle, compared to the tremendous, blinding light of the Shakespeares and Dantes who are incandescent enough to let the power from God's Niagara flow through them.

When Homer and Virgil invoked the Muses to write through them, it was not an idle request, but the deep yearning of their deepest souls. George Eliot said that she was a poor writer until she learned to let the "Not-self" do the writing. Joel Chandler Harris wrote his daughter in college that he was a mediocre writer in college till he let "the other fellow" lean over his shoulder and do the writing for him. And so it goes. Twenty years ago this theme was discussed in the *Pictorial Review*, in a debate between Zona Gale and Edna Ferber on "Are You a Factory or a Channel?"

That is the question for us to decide. Are the ductless glands factories or are they channels? Upon this depends a great deal. For if they are factories we need look no further. We must make our adjustment to them. But if they are channels we can look beyond them, to that source from whence their power comes, and try to make our adjustment to the great Creative Power at the center of the Universe. And the search for this power leads us to the very Kingdom of Heaven itself.

Jesus took very definite sides on this question. He hardly opened his mouth to speak without some such statement as this, "I speak not for myself, the Father who dwelleth in me, He doeth the works." One of the most outstanding statements on this theme ever made by him was when the seventy had returned from a period of marvelous miracle-working experiences, and they were telling in great elation of the wonderful power they had discovered in themselves for the casting out of demons. To this He said, "Rejoice not that the demons are subject unto you, but rejoice rather that your names are written in heaven." One might paraphrase this as follows: "Don't take too much credit for your imperial power over demons, or over anything else here in your own might, but rejoice rather that your own individual receiving sets (that is what Jesus meant by 'names') are connected up with the great Broadcasting Station in heaven."

Where has all of this discussion led us? Merely to face the fact that whether we approach this subject through Western study of the glands, or Eastern study of the soul centers, or whether we use the illustration of our modern house, we find all leading us back to a deeper conviction that the seven centers of the human body hook up somewhere or other, somehow or other, with the great Broadcasting Station of the GREAT OVER SOUL or the FATHER THAT IS IN HEAVEN. As all roads lead to Rome, so all study of the human glands leads us back to God. As Isaiah once said, "The head of Syria is Damascus, and the head of Damascus is (King) Rezin," so we can say, "The head of the human body is the glands, and the head of the glands is Jehovah, God of Hosts."